I AM A VICTIM OF
Amazing
GRACE

I AM A VICTIM OF
Amazing
GRACE

IDA HELTON

I Am a Victim of Amazing Grace
Copyright © 2020 by Ida Helton. All rights reserved.

No part of this publication may be reproduced, stored in a retrieval system or transmitted in any way by any means, electronic, mechanical, photocopy, recording or otherwise without the prior permission of the author except as provided by USA copyright law.

The opinions expressed by the author are not necessarily those of URLink Print and Media.

1603 Capitol Ave., Suite 310 Cheyenne, Wyoming USA 82001
1-888-980-6523 | admin@urlinkpublishing.com

URLink Print and Media is committed to excellence in the publishing industry.

Book design copyright © 2020 by URLink Print and Media. All rights reserved.

Published in the United States of America

ISBN 978-1-64753-201-7 (Paperback)
ISBN 978-1-64753-202-4 (Digital)

11.01.20

Because of His great love for us, God, who is rich in mercy, made us alive with Christ even when we were dead in transgressions – it is by *GRACE you have been saved.* *Ephesians 2:4-5 NIV*

By: Ida Helton

DEDICATION

Thank you to the Barn Fellowship for all your love and prayers. Your support could never be replaced.

Thank you to Marie Sims, without you my Awesome Joe and I would have been totally lost.

Thank you to Corey and Sandra Pitts, you brought me through, fed me, cleaned my house, did my laundry.. You were there for your grandmother and I will not forget.

Thank you to Dewayne and Crystal Pitts for staying with me through my recovery and making certain I eat every day. You did your mother very good.

Thank you to my Awesome Joe Helton for being the most supportive, positive, faithful and loving husband at this time. I love you with all my heart.

It's been said that most anyone can write a book, but how many have truly lived it? Ida Helton, author of "I Am a Victim of Amazing Grace", shares her journey with Follicular Non-Hodgkin's Lymphoma. Through her journey she has learned of God's gift of unmerited favor through His healing powers.

After being diagnosed with the incurable disease in 2013, Helton has experienced the power of God's ultimate restoration that He offers through the blood of Jesus. Her personal testimony documents journal entries over several months as she received treatment and watched as the cancer and tumors disappeared. While not cured, Helton claims her complete, divine healing, and in this autobiography of miracles, hope, and encouragement told through the perspective of Christianity, you'll find the faith to trust God for His promises and believe that nothing is stronger than His amazing grace.

In her journey and through her writing Ida echoes what the Holy Scriptures teach in Hebrews 11:6 that without faith it is impossible to please God. May this book encourage you, enlighten you and inspire you as you face life's trials.

Jerry Truett
Pastor of The Barn Fellowship

FOREWORD

When Mrs. Ida first asked me to write the foreword of her introduction to her first book, I was honored that she would choose me to do so, and also a bit scared. As I pondered as to how to do this section justice, I became slightly overwhelmed at the prospect of taking on such a task, even though I am a writer by trade, because I had never taken on such a responsibility and exactly how to accurately portray the amazing faith of this great woman of God, and furthermore the greatness of the God she serves so faithfully through an unquestioning and undoubting attitude.

I mean come on, several people will read my words trying to decide if this is a read they wish to purchase for themselves, or somebody they dearly love who may be in the darkest hours of life, just as you are at this very moment. I wondered exactly how I would convey just how amazing this woman's faith was during the toughest battle any human can face, and accurately explain exactly how valuable of a resource this book is in the scariest of times, and the majesty of the God it boasts about, while in the midst of a daunting struggle.

If you are reading this, you may also feel overwhelmed with choosing which book to purchase, surrounded by the thousands of self-help books flooding the market all swearing they are the roadmap to the discovery of internal peace and the end-all in the struggle with fear and uncertainty. To be clear, the book is the tool—God is the answer! Without God, any book purchase is simply a purchase of ink and paper neatly wrapped between two covers, and no more effective in your battle than any of the other options you see around you. You must seek God first during this journey to effectively become a true "victim" of God's grace.

I began and erased many versions of what you are now reading before I finally had my wife ask Mrs. Ida over to my house for a visit one Sunday morning after church. Although I have known Mrs. Ida for more than a decade, it was a daunting task, to say the least, to rightly represent the content encased within the following chapters, and the important message contained on these pages.

I was at ground zero as Mrs. Ida received a grim diagnosis and refused to give up on the faith that she held so dear as a disease attempted to devour her body and the medical community seemed to write off all hope. I was there when she refused to cry over a bad disease deemed uncurable and then as others wanted to mourn her fate as opposed to hold onto the same faith she ultimately found peace within. I was there when she laughed in the face of an ill-fated diagnosis.

The first thing that was throwing me off was the use of the word "victim" in the title--I am sure many of you grammar-Nazis out there noticed this right off the bat. If you are anything like me, this stuck out like a sore thumb—but after my conversation with Mrs. Ida on that Sunday morning, I knew exactly how I would proceed with this portion of the introduction to her book. My one and only question as I sought direction in how I would approach this valuable resource; why the use of the word "victim" in what some may think a contrary adjective to describe the love of our Lord and Savior, and the healing that took place in her life. As is true to her nature, and as I had assumed all along knowing her personally as I do—she knew exactly what she was doing, this was a totally intentional move, and in the process, she totally redefined the way I now look at the word "victim".

As Mrs. Ida recounted the event that inspired her choice in words, I too began to reflect on a time that I fell "victim" to God's grace. As she told me the story of a hurricane survivor being interviewed on a news program, bawling of her hardships caused by the hurricane and the displacement from her normal life through tears of misery, Mrs. Ida recalled this woman's surroundings used as a backdrop of the interview. Lavish furnishing in the background, the fact this woman was not sleeping in a homeless shelter or under a bridge, and the fact this woman missed the obvious signs around her that pointed to the fact she had been blessed in abundance although her life was not the same as it was prior to the tragedy stuck out to Mrs. Ida, and it struck her that although this woman on the news was telling a tale of hardship and destruction, her surroundings told a story of God's deliverance and protection.

I began to recall, as a man who has struggled with alcoholism and anger problems for most of my young adult life, how I would get lost in the "victimhood" of my own battles, and ignored the blessings of God that I would have never experience if I had not myself fallen "victim" to God's grace.

Many times, and I mean many times, I would go into a battle that threatened to uproot what I had considered good living conditions, a life that was now in peril of being lost forever—be it due to another DWI or some legal problem resulting from booze and a bad temper, or the loss of yet another job due to the bad economy—I would get lost in my obsession of what I risked losing and what I perceived as a normal comfortable life. I would ignore what God was doing around me while I was camping at rock bottom.

Man diagnosed me as bipolar, ADD, ADHD, and hypertensive. In a nutshell, medical professionals said I was totally screwed up in the mind, that mental disorders and addiction defined my life, and ultimately that medications were the only route to a "normal life"—but God disagreed and had a plan for my family that even I could not see. Because of faithful friends like Mrs. Ida, I never gave up hope in God and the deliverance He freely offers. I witnessed her battle with cancer, and her unbelievably upbeat approach to her situation, her undying faith in her Lord and Savior, and knew that God can, and will, make "victims" of us all if we will only get out of His way and allow Him to carry out His plan in our lives.

Whereas my situation was that of my own making and a product of idiotic habits of faulty coping mechanisms, and Mrs. Ida's was a battle with cancer and a grim prognosis from doctors through no fault of her own, the God we both serve is the same great and powerful God who wants more than anything to make us all "victims". I mean come on, we are all his creations, right? So, it would only be logical to conclude that he has ultimate control over our destinations and the paths our lives navigate during our time on this planet.

See, when we as humans get lost in the chaos, God finds ways to re-create our lives in amazing ways. It is totally possible to come out the other side of a struggle better than when the battle first began. My personal reconstruction happened as God opened doors for me to go back to college while on probation, when by law I should have been sitting out a sentence in a state prison for two felony DWIs, and abandon all mind-bending medications that negatively altered basic functions of my personality that had hindered any advancements in my professional life. In a situation where everybody was telling me I would spend years in prison, God laid the groundwork for me to eventually take over operations as Editor of our hometown newspaper, then a year later assume the seat of publisher when the paper sold to a corporate group out of state—a paper 5 years later my wife, Michelle, and I are in the process of taking ownership as I type this foreword. We now have two wonderful children, Corbin age 13 and Brailee age 9 (at the time of this writing), and I have not missed a single day of their childhood thanks to God's deliverance, and the undeniable fact that I am indeed a "victim" of God's great and unfailing love.

The hope that God offered as He was delivering me from a dire and bleakly predicted future (as seen in the eyes of man), was proof that He had a totally different future in mind for me and my family—one I would have never considered possible immersed in a battle that seemed unwinnable had it not been for the example set forth by truly God-inspired folks in my life, such as Mrs. Ida.

When Mrs. Ida was told she may not live to see another Christmas, she never wrote God off—quite to the contrary, SHE WROTE GOD UP! She literally wrote this book journaling her own experiences of God's grace throughout her journey, constructing this amazingly inspirational script to share the hope of our Creator and Savior so that others like yourself may find real peace in a battle marred by insurmountable odds.

Not all battles are the same, and the one you or your loved one is enduring at this very moment is unique in the manner that it is hard for others to relate from the observation deck, but God is in complete control--in this you must believe. Just look at the two I have shared in this brief introduction, mine being the product of man's sinful nature and my own idiocy while struggling with addiction, and her battle with cancer through no fault of her own. The message that needs to be gained as you search for hope in this tale of good news—our God is always the same, scripture is always true, and ANYBODY CAN BECOME A VICTIM OF GOD'S GRACE!

Keep up the good fight; keep your eyes upon Heaven; and keep God in everything! Become a victim of God's love, grace, and mercy!

Godspeed and God Bless,

Bert R. Fite
Publisher/Owner
Grand Saline Sun
Grand Saline, Texas

I AM A VICTIM OF AMAZING, WONDERFUL GRACE, and I do not care who likes it or does not like it. I don't care whether you agree with me. I want to wallow in the Grace of God, just like a pig wallows in his trough.

When Hurricane Harvey came on land in 2017, many people lost their homes, and all contents to the floods that came into Houston and south Texas, into southern Louisiana, and some parts of Mississippi. They were victims of a hurricane in need of rescue. The Federal Government; FEMA, Coast Guard, National Guard, even President Trump and Vice-President Pence came into Houston and Louisiana bringing US cabinet members with them to find out what they needed to help those who were so devastated.

When Hurricane Sandy came ashore in New Jersey, Governor Chris Christy and President Obama walked and surveyed the damage left behind. Again, many homes were destroyed, and residents lost all their precious belongings and memories to the disaster. They were victims of natural catastrophe.

I have watched in the past several years as the news reports on the downfall of yet another victim of hurricane Katrina. They tell us how very bad their luck is, and how terrible their situation still is, and they can never go back home.

I want you to understand, very carefully, here that I have as much compassion for those victims as anyone did. I have helped to establish new homes, through the Salvation Army and local churches. I have prayed with them just like everybody else did. I just think that after all this it is time to go on to the next story.

I am a victim, but not of a hurricane named Katrina. I am not a victim of rape or murder. I am not a victim of robbery. I am not a victim of the stock market crash.

The same is true for those left behind after the twin towers fell in New York on September 11, 2001. I was in shock for several days. I could not eat or drink; the pain flowed in my gut as if I had been there. I prayed, on my knees for those survivors and for the survivors of the victims. I still hurt so badly, deep inside, that I want to upchuck at the memories of what happened that day. I was in Terrell, Texas and had to watch all of this unfold on national television, as most of us did. Our world came to a screeching halt for about 2 weeks before we could get up and go on. My pain was for those left behind and for those who died. My pain was for them, and it was also for me, because I could for the first time see that our enemy was very real, and that he had attacked on our own soil. I cried out to God for our nation's leaders to do the right thing in this situation. I think we should make it a National Day of Remembrance, every year. And I think that we should all come to a screeching halt at that time every year… the moment that we heard the news.

What I don't want to see is people wallowing and profiting off of their misery for the next hundred years. I hate to see people actually dwelling on their misery. Why can't we focus on the good that is left behind and carry on.

My Bible says we should 'press forward' to those things which are ahead, (Philippians 3:14). We should be trying to dig ourselves out, focusing on those things which are to come. Thank God for that Amazing Grace that heals all wounds and wipes away every tear. It is time we stopped wallowing in our VICTIM-HOOD, and began to praise God for his Amazing Grace.

He lives, He is alive and because of that I am healed, forgiven and preparing to join Him in a heavenly home where no tears will ever flow again.

I didn't lose a lot in the stock market fall a few years ago, because I didn't have a lot to lose. I could tell you that my financial times are hard. But what I prefer to tell you is that because I believe in Him, because I am a victim of His Amazing Grace, then I don't have to worry about these things, because He is my Provider, my Comforter, my best Friend. I choose to wallow in His Grace and to let others do the same.

Now, before I continue, I will tell you that we have a trucking company. In September 2005, one of our drivers died in the tractor he was driving. He passed in his sleep and no one else was hurt; he just didn't wake up to carry on with his work. When we couldn't reach him, when his spouse could not reach him by telephone, we had to send someone out to look for him. He had not been driving for us very long, and we didn't know him very well, but this was not what I prayed for him and his family. The truck he was driving sat for several months, with no driver. The revenue potential from that equipment was swallowed up in death.

My step-son died in November 2005, just a few months later. What a horrible blow for all of us. Because we are a truck driving family (we had five rigs at that time), and because my husband and his family are very respected and loved by those in this industry, our business came to a halt for several days. Joe was home for three weeks, while his truck sat and made no revenue. One driver went home with a sinus infection which had settled in his eyes and missed several weeks of work. Another driver went home and sat for four weeks after passing a kidney stone. The revenue potential of our business was swallowed up in death, this all happened at the same time, within just two weeks.

It was a tremendous blow to our finances; our savings were depleted. Our bills kept on arriving. For the first time in eleven years, the payments started going out two or three weeks late, instead of two or three weeks early. Our credit cards were maxed out from trying to reach expenses which have to be paid. When the trucks are your livelihood, then you must make sure they are road-ready at all times. If they sit for a few weeks, then your financial situation becomes a monster which has been swallowed up in death.

My health has taken a beating. I have been diagnosed with Fibromyalgia, and with Dysmetabolic Syndrome. For weeks, I sat in my house engulfed with pain. I could not stand up from a sitting position without excruciating pain. My muscles did not want to work. They would not cooperate with me. When I finally did get up, I couldn't straighten up. I was in too much pain. My health was swallowed up in the results of death. (I believe that I allowed myself to concentrate too much on the status of our business and not on my health and welfare, forgetting that Christ died for my healing.)

Through it all, we have purchased more trucks, taken on new drivers. We have made aggressive decisions to change our business. I have visited several doctors trying to get healthy. I stay home and take care of the office and manage the business from my home. My office has suffered because of my illness and now I have hired help to get it all straightened out. Our business and our livelihood have fallen victim to the deaths of two men. Is death, then, trying to swallow us up?

I remember that when my Daddy died I lived right around the corner from the cemetery, less than a mile from where we laid him to rest. I had to drive past his grave to go into town and come past it again on the way out of town. I stayed there for four more years. I drove past that cemetery every day at least twice. I got so I had to turn my head the other way. It was always there. My mother would ask me if I had been to the cemetery lately, and I would say "every day." I knew I had to get away, to stop this wallowing, but there was no other way to get out of our subdivision except to drive past that cemetery. Finally, I just had to move away. I knew all the facts. I really did not believe that he was there, and I didn't actively cry and all that stuff, I just couldn't force myself to drive past there anymore. I realize now that I was wallowing in my daddy's death.

You bet it is trying to swallow us up. After all, what is death? It is separation from family and life. Our enemy's assignment toward us is to steal, kill and destroy. If he can force us to wallow in the death then he can succeed very easily. I pray that the driver knew Christ as his savior. I know that Richard, our son, knew him.

I have given much thought to this over the past several months. Our business is falling victim to the circumstances around us. We have to fight on a daily basis to pay our bills, and to keep the creditors from our door step.

I have spent many days on my knees asking God what we should do next. I pray before I pay bills, because I know that if I do it wrong we could lose something to repossession.

I do not want to wallow in my circumstances. I do not want to wallow in death. I want to wallow in the Victory that I have through Jesus Christ.

I could tell you how horribly all of this has affected us, but I do not want to wallow in the dirt as a VICTIM of my circumstances. I want to rise up and say that I am a certified, bonified VICTIM of AMAZING GRACE.

Jesus Christ came to earth as a baby; he lived the life of a human. He was born of a virgin, crucified on a cross for me, and then He went into hell and took the keys to life right out of Satan's hands. Having done so, He rose again to walk and talk with the disciples, and a few chosen others, before being resurrected into Heaven to sit at the right hand of God.

He lives there to make intercession for me and you. That is Amazing Grace.

He knew me before I was conceived in my mother's womb. He knew that I would need a Savior, and He came for me. Every stripe that He took with that cat of nine tails was for me, for my healing. Every drop of blood that He shed was for my salvation. He knew me, and He loved me enough to do that for me. What a lovely thought, Amazing Grace.

And, He didn't just do all of that for me, it was for you also. He knew us long before our parents did. He knew the choices we would make, and loved us enough to allow us to make them. It is called Amazing Grace.

Jesus Christ, the most amazing gift our Father could have given us, and He did it all for our healing, our salvation, our redemption. Don't let anybody tell you differently.

Yeah, at first glance this chapter sounds like we are victims of something truly horrible, but if you will allow me—I will show you the Grace of which we are victims. I want you to know before I start that I have authority and knowledge of what it is like to experience these things. I want you to understand that I know where you are. I have been there (as we used to say, 'bought the t-shirt, wore it out, gave it away).

Ida Helton
Jan 16, 2013

The telephone rang on the 18th of December 2012. I saw it was a Tyler number before I answered but did not recognize it. I had a Mammogram done on December 4th and had been waiting for results. The nurse introduced herself and told me the doctor had found some 'abnormalities' and wanted further testing. I tried to put it off until after

Christmas, but they would have none of that and we finally settled on an appointment the morning of the 20th.

My husband, Awesome Joe, was home at the time and he drove me down. I sat in that lobby with several women in various stage of dress with hospital gowns on, until they called me back. I kept thinking, 'we're all here for the same reason'. Finally, they called me back. 6 more pictures of the left breast and some of them hurt, before asking me to wait in the lobby again.

Finally, they called me back for the Sonogram. The lady introduced herself, (they all do, never been treated better) and explained to me that she was going to do some Sonogram work before calling the doctor in. (WHAT?) She dug and dug, finally found the pictures she wanted, marked them and then called him.

It's obvious by now that something is very wrong. He looks at her markings, moves out, moves back in and wants to look at the right breast also. Now, I'm getting scared. I turned so he could look, but he's looking at the underarm.

Finally, he stops, he explains to me that there is a dense something or other in the left breast and he wants to do a biopsy, but there is also something in the underarm on the right side. "Double Biopsy" he says.

Since Christmas is coming, and we all have plans he finally says 'this has gone far enough that waiting 2 more weeks isn't going to make any difference, so they scheduled a GUIDED NEEDLE BIOPSY for January 8th.

I probably don't have to tell you that I ran to my husband's arms and told him what had been said before pulling myself up. I called our pastor and a few good prayer partners and told them what was going on. One thing is for sure, I am not going into that without prayer warriors behind me.

My son drove me in for the biopsy, Awesome Joe was back on the road, and we came home and prayed for good results.

God doesn't always answer us the way we want. At 9:05 am on Thursday January 10, 2013, Dr. Lee called to tell me the results are in. It is not breast cancer as they thought; **IT** is Follicular Non-Hodgkin's Lymphoma. When I started to ask him questions, he told me he was referring me to an Oncologist and that his office would set it up and they would call me back.

The appointment was made with Dr Yimer, at the Tyler Cancer Center, and we were there on Tuesday, the 15th. They did blood work, and I saw him and he ordered a CT scan so he can see where it is. He said his preliminary is Grade 2 (Intermediate) and that he thinks I am in early stages, but he cannot be sure until the tests are returned.

During the past few days, I have looked at several support groups. On one website, the first thing I saw was a person talking about how their brother had died within 7 years of diagnoses. While I understand they need support, it was the last thing I wanted to see. Then I went to www.lls.org/ntx and they have a wealth of resources, but nothing going in DFW.

I have this disease, it is now a part of me, but does that mean I have to live according to the rules of Leukemia/Lymphoma? I am a Christian, I believe in healing, and I believe that everything that happens to us is for a reason. I am ready to see what my Heavenly Father has for me next.

This morning on Facebook, I saw a post that said, "YOU ARE GOING TO WANT TO GIVE UP. DON'T" I typed it up and posted it on my wall. I am looking for people who have positive messages and who won't give up

just because some doctor says it, or because of what the tests say, or because you are tired. I want to talk to other people who are here, but not the quitters. I want people who believe in HIS HEALING POWER to encourage me.
    and so... THE JOURNEY BEGINS.

CHAPTER TWO

Amazing Grace how sweet the sound… A song the holy angels cannot sing.

How long has it actually been since you looked to see if you had anything to be thankful for? We tend to get comfortable in our love for the Lord, we allow ourselves to get okay with a few moments of prayer a day, and if we forgot to read our Bible then we can just do it tomorrow. It is easy to slump off of our routine one or two days, and then to break the habit.

He wants our full attention. He wants us to pay attention. He wants to be the center of our purpose and from that perspective, He is able to do exceeding abundantly above all we ask or think (Ephesians 4:19).

Satan wants us to forget to pray today, or to just be too busy; because if we forget today, he can use that to his advantage in the battle against us. He looks for every weak spot. He knows us almost as well as our Father God does. He hits at the knees when they are unprotected, but he also knows how to go for the elbows. His assignment is to 'Steal, Kill, Destroy' those whom he can. He roams throughout the earth, seeking those whom he may devour (1 Peter 5:8).

We are responsible for staying in tune with the Holy Spirit, for being ever attentive to His guidance, and without His guidance and wisdom we can fall victim so quickly to the wiles of the evil one.

It is apparent that we need Amazing Grace to withstand the attacks which are launched at us. Let us take a look back at some of the people in the Old and New Testament who survived because of the Amazing Grace our Father extends.

The most apparent warfare was against Job, poor Job, who was such a strong man of faith that Satan had to go and ask God for permission to torture him. In Job 1, we see that Job was blameless, a man of complete integrity. He feared God and stayed away from evil. (NLT) He was very wealthy and had a large family. Satan was jealous, and he went and asked permission to try Job. In the New Living Translation, we see him coming before the Lord. He says, 'You have always protected him and his home and his property from harm. You have made him prosperous in everything he does... But (if you) take everything he has, he will surely curse you to your face.'

God granted permission for Satan to try and test Job. "Do whatever you want with everything he possesses, but don't harm Job physically."

In Chapter 1, verse 21, we see Job's response to the first attack. "The Lord gave me everything I had, and the Lord has taken it away. Praise the name of the Lord."

Drop on down to verse 6, chapter 2 and you will see that God allows another attack, "Do with him as you please, but spare his life." Then Job was attacked with boils from head to foot. Verse 10 tells us that Job was still unwilling to say anything wrong about God. He continued to praise the Father.

As you read on in this short book, you will see that Job had advice from all his friends and his wife. But yet, he trusted God. There was a period where he questioned God, but he still knew that God was all powerful. In chapter 42, Job begins by saying, 'I know that you can do anything, and no one can stop you.'

The end result is well known, after Job had been tested, after he had lost everything, after he had been covered by boils from head to toe, when God healed and restored him he did it royally. 'When Job prayed for his friends, the Lord restored his fortunes. In fact, the Lord gave him twice as much as before... "So, the Lord blessed Job in the second half of his life even more than in the beginning" (Job 42:10-12). It was Amazing Grace which restored Job's fortune and family. There can be no doubt about it.

Look at the Israelite children when they came to the Red Sea. They moaned and grumbled, but God showed his Amazing Grace by parting the sea and they crossed over on dry ground. God was not finished yet. He waited until all the Egyptian soldiers were in the midst of that river before allowing the waters to fall and to swallow them up.

Was it not Amazing Grace which fed the children of Israel manna from Heaven while they walked the desert for forty years? Was it not Amazing Grace which allowed David to slay a giant with a slingshot and a small stone?

In the New Testament, when Paul and Silas were thrown in jail, was it not Amazing Grace that allowed the walls to collapse as they began to sing praises to God on High? Is it not Amazing Grace which saves us?

Amazing Grace how sweet the sound, that saved a wretch like me.

We have to understand the Grace which He wrought for us in order to become a victim of it. I have to work this out. If I become victim of the circumstances around me, and of the attacks that Satan throws my way, then I am just a victim. But, what if I were to allow Him to help me through this? What could actually happen were I to stand strong in His promises and allow Him to take charge of the situation, whilst I turn my attention to praising Him and to searching for His purpose in my life? I decided to give it a try. Just like that, turn my back on the problem and look Heaven-ward and see if He can turn the situation around.

Now, that decision is pretty easy for me, I've practiced it a lot in my sixty years. What was hard was getting my husband and a few others involved.

See, several years ago, I knew we needed a big miracle. I was in bad shape, and so was the business. I called our daughter and asked her to join me in 'Forty Days of Prayer'. She quickly agreed. And so, we started to meet by telephone each day, and one of us would read the Scriptures, and we would discuss them as we did so. The other would pray. Now, I like this kind of warfare, because it pits two of us and gives us strength.

Then my husband stayed home for a week. Hallelujah, he stayed home. He asked what we were doing and I told him. He began to join in our discussion and to join us for prayer. Wow, it didn't take long. Then the music in our house changed a little bit. Not the quiet stuff we usually play, but I am now blasting praises into the air. Suddenly, my husband is holding my hand again and we are in agreement as to what we need. We begin to worship and to allow Him to have the problems.

Ecclesiastes 4:9 says "Two are better than one, because together they can work effectively. If one of them falls down, the other can help him up" (Ecclesiastes 4:9 NIV). Two people can resist an attack that would defeat one person alone. A rope made of three cords is hard to break.

We stand together and ask God to meet our needs in accordance with His plan and purpose for us. We offer Him praise together and then we go on with our day, as usual, and wait to see what happens. One thing is for sure, we pay our tithe and we give what we can and what we feel led to give. I refuse to let the devourer take from me anything that God does not allow him to have (Malachi 3).

After a few days, my husband and I are in agreement that nothing is going to happen here which God does not allow. IF it does not destroy us then it will make us stronger. We are in agreement that If God be for us then nothing can stand against us that He does not allow. How can we fail? Even failure in our business would not be failure. It would be allowing ourselves to be used of God and to allow His purpose free reign in our lives.

Apparently, He wants us to stand. And so, we stand firm in the belief that He can fix. He has blessed us to triple the business in three years. We have been aggressive and bold in the expansion. Now it is time to let the business take care of us for a while. For that to happen, we must have drivers in all the trucks, and the freight must be there to pull. We must allow God to weed out those things which are set to destroy us (drivers who are not helping us and vehicles which are costing too much to operate). Even our checkbooks must be allowed to meet His scrutiny. Are we giving enough? Are we planting our seed in good, fertile ground?

It is exceedingly hard to wake up on a Monday morning and realize that three of the six trucks do not have drivers. One has bought his own truck. One has been dealing with some severe health problems and has given notice and worked his time out and left. The last has refused to take a drug screen and simply parked his truck in the drive and left us a note. (Wow, I didn't see that one coming.) Three trucks without drivers means half our revenue potential is not working.

What is awesome in that situation is that by Monday of the next week, you have drivers headed to orientation and ready to drive this weekend. And one of those drivers is a TEAM, with double the revenue potential. That is how God works things out. That is Amazing Grace.

And even if they don't all work out, we know that God is in control, and we can leave the worrying to Him and we can relax in His Grace.

CHAPTER THREE

Amazing Grace.... It's a song the holy angels cannot sing.

When God was doing all His creating, He created man in his own image. Now the Bible does not say that about angels. In fact, we are given vivid descriptions of angels in the personage of Lucifer, the chief musician, and also in the book of Revelation. Angels were to worship Him, to Praise Him. He created man in his own image. You and me, He created us to be like Him.

God created man in His own image so that He would have someone to communicate with. We are told that He walked daily in the garden with Adam. He dearly wanted someone with whom He could just communicate. It would be very easy for me to be jealous of Adam and Eve. They had it all, and all they had to do was abstain from eating the fruit of one tree. They could walk with God daily in the garden. They could talk to Him one on one. I am not a jealous person at all, but the thought of what they had really pains me. I would love to be the one who is free to walk and talk with God (face to face) on a daily basis.

These two didn't even have to wonder about the next day, all they were required to do was walk and talk with God, their creator, who loved them dearly. How harsh and painful that must have been for God, their Father, to realize that they wanted that fruit more than they wanted the communication with Him. (He already knew they would fall, that's why He made the plan of Salvation, His Only Son for the future redemption of man.)

What Grace must abound in the Father that He would allow them to live and procreate, after their fall.

I personally like the idea that Amazing Grace will take us all home to dwell with Him forever in Heaven, and that we don't have to do anything to EARN this gift, we simply must believe and confess with our mouths that Jesus is the Christ, and that He lived and died and was resurrected for our sins; and, of course, that He now sits at the right hand of the Father ever making intercession for us. If we have done that then we are forgiven and ready to live forever with Him. You can't work hard enough to earn it, and you can't slide in without the proper action. It is a gift freely given, we simply must believe.

The Israelite children left out of Egypt with all the gold and silver the people could throw at them. Shortly after leaving Egypt they were on the run. The Egyptians were following them, or as we say, in hot pursuit. They had the Red Sea in front of them, and Pharaoh's army behind them. The Bible tells us there were 450 thousand men, not counting the women and children. That means there were probably over one million Israelites. They started to moan and groan, 'It would have been better to have been left in Egypt to die.'

God had mercy on those people. They were truly chosen by Him. He simply said "Stand still and see the Glory of the Lord."

Imagine, if you will, the sight of one million people standing still and quiet with the Lord. They were all waiting for Him to appear. As the crowd grew still, mothers holding the small children to keep them still and quiet. Older children were helping and holding on to the younger ones. We can't get a crowd of twenty to be still and quiet, it is almost impossible. And they didn't have police and guards; they didn't have a massive sound system. They had a huge crowd and maybe the equivalent of our modern-day bullhorn. But they all got quiet and still. Moses lifted that staff out over the waters and they began to part. The waters rose up into the air, forming two walls approximately 50 feet high and rolled back up onto them. We are told that the Children of Israel were able to cross over immediately on dry land. They didn't even get their feet wet.

How much grace and mercy did that take? But, God was not finished yet. The next passage tells us that He waited until all those Egyptians were in the dried-up river bed before dropping the two walls of water back down on them. It says that they were all destroyed. The Israelite Children were saved by one fell swoop of the Master's hand.

I get really excited when I think about all the miracles recorded in the Bible. Here we see the Israelite children being the VICTIMS OF AMAZING GRACE.

Look further, at the stories of Gideon, in Judges 6 and 7. Gideon was not a well-known man, but he was a ruler of Israel for a period of approximately 40 years. When he first began to lead the Israelites, he amassed an army of 32,000 men to overtake the Midianites and the Amalekites. Their armies were huge. God said, no, that was too many men. If Gideon led 32,000 men into battle then the people would say it was the army that freed them. They worked out for 22,000 men to return to their homes. God told Gideon that was still too many men. He had Gideon lead them to a river, and to watch the men drink water from the river. He was to keep only those who used their hands to scoop and drink the water. He was down to 300 men.

It would have been very easy for Gideon (and any other person in that same situation) to have said, "300 men to fight that army. No way, I will just stand here and wallow in our defeat." But Gideon had a vision of what was to come. He trusted the Lord to give him the Amazing Grace to overcome. Even those 300 men trusted Gideon to lead them. They chose to wallow in the victory.

This is where we begin to develop our faith. And to do that you must understand what faith really is…

FAITH

FAITH is FULLY AND IMPLICITLY TRUSTING HIM

You've got to have faith. Each and every one of us is given a measure of faith the size of a tiny mustard seed. That's all you need to begin with. It's enough. It is actually more than enough. The Bible tells us that "faith cometh by hearing and hearing by the Word of God" (Romans 10:17 KJV).

First, it is important to understand that you can't even begin to accept Salvation until you have received that faith. When you truly believe that Jesus Christ is the Son of God, that He was born of a virgin, was crucified, and rose again on the third day, and that He now sits at the Father's right hand ever making intercession for us, then you have the faith that is required to sincerely ask Him into your heart, to forgive your sins and to give you eternal life. That eternal life is already yours. Jesus bought it with His life, and then He went into the bowels of Hell and fought the devil and won the battle, taking the keys to life and death from his hands. He rose again, triumphant to walk on this earth again, and then was ascended to His throne. When you believe this, it is easy to ask Him into your life.

After we are saved, then God wants us to expand our faith. "Faith cometh by hearing and hearing by the Word of God" (Romans 10:17 KJV). We are told to not "forsake the assembling of ourselves together" (Hebrews 10:25 KJV). As you meet with other believers, as you hear their testimony, as you receive the Word of God into your heart, your faith will grow. As your faith grows, you will begin to understand that you can ask Him for whatever you need, and then one day you will come to the realization that your needs are already met. Then, you can start praying for the things you desire.

It is important to understand that as your mind is transformed by the Word, as your heart conforms to the Word, then your desires will begin to line up with Christ's desire for your life (Romans 12-2). Soon, you will begin to see that your desires are His desires, and because they have meshed, then He will direct your path.

Here is where you fully understand the faith that is imparted to you. FAITH is Fully And Implicitly Trusting Him. You are now at a point, as I have been for years, that everything that happens is for a reason and you simply need to line your life up with His Word for you to see perfection.

I am not talking about being perfect in the flesh, no man can be perfect. I am talking about the act of being made perfect before an almighty, all powerful, omniscient, omnipresent God. A God who loves you enough, before you were ever even thought of here on this earth, to make a perfect plan for your Salvation, and for you to live eternally with Him, in total perfection.

What, you ask, is faith? FAITH is Fully And Implicitly Trusting Him.

Now that you have a better understanding of faith, hopefully, it is time to put it into action.

Everything that slows you down or gets in your way, should become a reason to praise Him, not a reason to curse your fellow men or become angry.

You said that car in front of you was running 20 mph in a 40-mile zone and you couldn't get around him because of the traffic. Behind you the cars are stacking up and you just want out of the mess. Now, me, I try to remember to say, "Thank you, Lord, I know we are going slowly for a purpose." Someone else might be blowing their horn, tapping on the wheel, goosing the engine. You might even be making weird gestures in the air directed at the car ahead and its ever-weary driver. STOP. Begin to praise the Lord. In a few minutes you will understand that the vehicles in front of you, up there where you were supposed to be, were involved in an accident. Now you can say, "There but for the Grace of God go I." It could have been you. Maybe, just maybe, God put that slow car in front of you for that very reason.

Or, maybe it's a spiritual battle to keep you from being where you need to be.

One thing I know for sure, if you start thanking God for it, instead of blaming Him and everyone around you, once you start praising Him, then if it is a spiritual battle the enemy will have to flee. He can't stay where the Spirit of Almighty God is. He will leave, and you can return to normal.

I will show you more of this as we work through the balance of this book.

CHAPTER FOUR

PROGRAMMED TO TALK DEFEAT

I challenge you to watch any of the television channels available today, aside from the faith-based programming on Daystar and TBN and others like them, for a period of 24 hours. Every time you hear a negative voice, or commercial, every time someone speaks the horrible truth of our status today, mark it down. Take note of how much is there. At the end of your day, count the marks. If you dare, compare each negative remark to what the Bible might say to the circumstance.

In the few days between the need for more tests, and the diagnosis of cancer, my husband (Awesome Joe) and I laughed and talked about the situation. I told him I had to laugh. I laughingly told him he was going to get a new wife and that he could pick my hair, because I would lose all my hair, and then I would lose a lot of weight. The day the doctor began to describe my treatment; I looked at my Awesome Joe and said, "Sorry, darling, that means you are stuck with me." I did not lose my hair. I did not lose a single pound. He gets to keep me just like I am.

When the diagnosis was pronounced, I simply said, "Absolutely no negatives." Cancer is a large battle emotionally. I knew without asking that I needed to hear the positive.

My brain could come up with enough horrible stuff. I never spoke it aloud.

We must program ourselves differently.

I went to several support sites. Every single time I connected, people were moaning, sharing horror stories of what had happened to them or to their family member. I couldn't even say CANCER out loud. I continually told people I had Lymphoma, never cancer.

I was around four months into the treatment when one of my friends brought me a visitor. As we talked, she looked at her friend and asked her how I looked. I was shocked. Her friend looked at me and said, "She looks fine to me. Why?" It was at that point, my friend looked at her and said, "She is eaten up with cancer."

I was shocked. I hadn't used that word. I had to back up and rethink my position. I let it bother me for a few days. I had nightmares about it. This "C" was chasing me around like the little yellow orb in the Pac Man game. He was chomping at me and taking small portions of my body.

I really had to shake myself awake. I got up and starting shouting, in the middle of the night, "I am not eaten up with cancer." I shouted it over and over. Finally, I turned on the computer, got on Facebook and started the mantra (like the old song where you sing b-i-n-g-o). "I am not eaten up with cancer. I am not ..... with cancer. I am not .... Cancer. I am ... . Cancer. I .. .. Cancer. I .. .. I am fully healed in Jesus Name."

This may sound silly to you. But I had to get that out of my mind. I simply had to. I am NOT a victim of cancer. I am not a victim of anything except Amazing Grace. I am a Victim of Amazing Grace.

My mind is programmed. I read the Scripture. I tell myself the best that can happen. I repeat over and over, I am a Victim of Amazing Grace.

Did you hear the commercials for the cancer treatment places? I really love these. 'I didn't know what to do.' 'I didn't know how to...' 'I was so scared.' Please. I don't understand how everyone who has cancer (or Aids, or Fibromyalgia, or Diabetes) can be portrayed as such needy people. We are not. We have a Father in Heaven who has made a blood covenant with us and we can rely on His Word.

If you are a Christian, if you are a believer, then you should be able to confront every situation in your life with the same faith. Once you become a believer, you are covered by a covenant that God made with Abraham in Deuteronomy 28. The first 15 verses of that chapter tell us the blessings that we can claim, should we just follow the Word of God, and be obedient. The last part of the chapter tells us the penalties for not being obedient. I prefer, for the purpose of this manuscript to dwell on the blessings.

My son is in his forties. My oldest grandson is 22 years old. There are 3 other grandchildren. I can't tell you they live their lives for the Lord, but I can tell you they will come. I have a promise in Proverbs 22:6 that if I raise my children in the way the Lord would have them to grow up, then when they are old they won't go away from it. I know they will return. In Deuteronomy 28:4, it says that "even the fruit of my body will be blessed." That's my children and grandchildren.

My daughter-in-law called me a few years ago. My son had appendicitis, they had to do surgery. Because of complications during the process, he was off work for over 3 months. When she called me, they were out of food, no money for utilities and didn't know what to do. She was very scared. Upon hanging up the phone from her, I pulled my car over to the side of the road. I called upon my Father for an answer. I first allowed myself to be judged, to ask if I was doing all He had asked of me. And then, after making sure He had permission to change me if that was what was needed, I reminded God of His covenant with Abraham. I am a direct descendant of Abraham, because I have Jesus blood. I reminded Him that if I was doing all that I was supposed to do, if I was correct, then He and I have a blood covenant and He is responsible for blessing my children. I didn't say it arrogantly. I asked humbly for correction if I needed it, and then I asked Him why my kids were not blessed.

She called back about three hours later and said, "You are not going to believe this." The elderly lady across the street had become a vegetarian. Her grown children were trying to force her to eat meat; she came home to find three grocery bags full of meat which she brought across to Libby with pleasure. She told Libby she was chosen because she saw how many children were always there and that Libby must be good to the kids. So, God used her adult children to bless Libby and Dewayne. That's His blood covenant with us. We only need claim it.

In the past few months, I have watched my grandson come to a blessing. Everything the devil meant for his destruction, God turned it and used it for Corey's good. Corey and Sandra were working in a donut shop. She worked every day, 4 to 5 hours a day, and he worked 3 days for 5 hours. The money was not good, but they were happy and looking forward to him going to full time quickly. Instead, someone decided to gossip and spread destruction. Both lost their jobs very fast. What happened next was nothing short of a miracle. My phone rang, someone looking for my son. When they told me for what I told them Dewayne can't do that. I said Corey was available and would call them back. This phone call turned into a full time, hard-working position where they can work together, and make good money. They will be moving into a house very soon. Corey and Sandra are blessed because Corey is the fruit of my body, and I am trying to do all that God has commanded me to do. That's God's blood covenant with me through Abraham.

Praising God gives me strength
Jan 22, 2013 11:54am

Today I am simply reading His Word and listening to praise music. The bird is singing with it. I am strong because He is with me. I am protected by His angels flying over and around me to make sure nothing can harm me. I dwell in the secret place of the Most High (Psalm 91), I abide in the shadow of the Almighty, and because I do no evil can befall me.

There is healing in the Name of Jesus, power in the Name of Jesus.

I was shocked by the diagnosis, but everything has come in baby steps and I have time to get used to the next thing before it comes. I thank my God for that, because if this had all come at me in a day or two I would have been screaming. Now I know more of what is coming. He knew how to present it to me.

This is not something they can cut out; it's all over the trunk of my body. Yesterday, when they went to install the PICC they wanted to know where it is. I pointed at the shoulder top and then to top of my legs and said, "Here to here, take your pick." They laughed with me, not at me. Then they got serious, and the doctor said, "You're serious." I said yes. They were all shocked that I was in such a good mood about it. No reason to get gloomy.

God is on His throne and ALL is well with my soul. He knew me before I was born. He wrote my life story. I just want to know that the battle is not in vain and that someone watching me will come to know the Son of God and the Father because of my testimony.

So far as treatment, I am waiting for insurance approval to start the Chemo. Pray it comes soon. Guess I watch too many kids shows, because Shrek would say, "Let's get this party started now."

Awesome is coming home
Jan 22, 2013 6:41pm

My wonderful husband will be here in just a few minutes. I am so happy to see him, and I need his arms.

Did you ever try to wrap an arm with Saran Wrap to keep it from getting wet? Such contortions. I have this PICC and it can't get wet. Have to wrap it to keep it dry in the shower. It took me three times to get it covered. I kept thinking, "All I want to do is wash my body." It was really funny.

Some things you have to learn. I'm going to have the PICC for at least 6 months. Can't wait that long to shower. HAHAHAHA

God is in the simple things
Jan 23, 2013 9:25am

My mom has reminded me, "ALL things work together for good to those who Love the Lord and are called according to His Purpose" (Romans 8:28, NKJV). I guess that about covers it.

The PICC was uncomfortable last night so think I will just rest today and let it heal in place (that's what Awesome Joe says it needs). Awesome Joe said I did way too much yesterday and he scolded me for it. Now he wants me up and at it.

Have a blessed day.

Jan 23, 2013 2:17pm
Angels and Roses

Every now and then we all have a little bit of a rough day. There you are. But I have a picture hanging on my wall that says, "My grace is sufficient for thee, for my strength is made perfect in weakness." (2 Corinthians 12:9, KJV).

Hallelujah, I don't have to worry about it. He is in complete charge. Mrs. Kim Allen taught the youth at Brookside Baptist Church to LET GO... LET GOD. I can relate to that, because there are things I am finding I just can't do (Like wrap my arm with Saran Wrap, HAHA) but I am sure glad that Awesome Joe is here today. I told him early, I work in small spurts of energy. He decided it was time to encourage me, thus the lovely roses from my beloved.

It helps more than you know to have a spouse and children who understand and try to help as much as they can. And who listen when the Spirit moves them to encourage and not to baby me.

I have these little angels all over my house that people have given me. They are night lights; they hang on the wall, just little trinkets, and some beautiful gifts and music boxes. I feel like they are all reminding me that God is watching out for me and that He cares for me. They offer encouragement during the hard times.

House computers
By Ida Helton — Jan 24, 2013 9:40am

The internet is not working at home. Please forgive simple typos.

I called the Oncologist office this morning and am scheduled to be there at 1:30 today. They are going to look at the PICC line and try to see why there is so much pain. I woke up to much worse this morning. I really think they should have given me an antibiotic upon insertion. I have a low-grade temperature. Awesome Joe is making me eat, trying to take good care of me. He really is God's greatest gift to me. I was in my office and found a small angel pin for my shoulder. I have probably had it for several years, and now it's time to wear it. The card reads "He gives His angels charge over me, to keep me in all my ways." Awesome Joe wrapped my arm this morning. He came with foil. Of course, that won't work. Then, he brought the Saran Wrap. He took it out of the box and wrapped it round and round. Finally, he decided it was done and put it back in the box to cut it. As he was leaving the room, he said, "Have to get you a pallet wrap machine. That'll keep you dry." That man has the funniest ideas. I guess that's why I love him so much.

Jesus, I will trust in You alone
Jan 25, 2013 7:17am

You are my hiding place, I will trust in You. Let the weak say I am strong in the strength of the Lord. I will trust in You.

My sister, Martha, and I were talking late last night. I believe this really hit her hard because she lives in Michigan and can't be here to help and comfort me. She can't check on me like she wants to. Last time I talked to her she was crying, and I was telling her to smile and understand that nothing is going to happen to me unless God allows it. She came at me with a Faith devotional last night and was quoting Scriptures from Hebrews and Psalms, and so many others. Our parents taught us faith to walk through any fire untouched. We will come through this.

She really helped me because she was ready for me last night. We talked for over an hour. I love her and miss her, but her life is there with another Awesome Joe (she met him after I found out how good a Joe can actually be).

Today, let yourselves be encouraged with the knowledge that the whole earth is filled with the Glory of God, and ask Him to show you His glory.

I am on my way back to Tyler in less than an hour, and I pray I will touch someone there.

Arm/PICC feels better
Jan 25, 2013 12:29pm

They have now re-wrapped it (my arm) and put heavy pressure stockinet on it to reduce any swelling and to help the incision to heal. Thank God, she said there is nothing wrong with it except the heavy bandaging had been on it too long, causing it to be really sore. She also said that as it heals I will be much freer to use the arm. NOW I GET IT.

Anyway, having the wisdom that I asked God for in this situation, I am going to bed for a while.

Love you all.

These are my journal posts. I want you to see that I never gave up, I never cried. I tried to let the Lord use me to bless others, no matter what the outcome. I am going to share them all, or at least most of them. One thing I already know is that God has used my testimony to help at least four other people overcome their own cancer. He is the Author and the Finisher of my faith and it is only for His Glory that I am here.

We were praying about the insurance situation because I still was not approved for the chemo treatments. We needed a miracle. We needed a few miracles. It took three weeks to get that approval.

In the meantime, Joe was trying to drive his truck. He called from Kingman, Arizona to tell me the turbo in the truck had blown. We didn't have anything left. I told him not to fret. God has a plan. He got up the next morning and called the company we are leased to and they told him he could rent a truck, but would need to get to Phoenix to pick it up. That worked great because the truck was financed through a company in Phoenix. He dropped the trailer in Kingman and drove to Phoenix in slow motion to take the truck to the Volvo dealership there. Instead of calling, he drove to the finance company's office. He walked in and was able to talk to them. They refinanced the truck and wrote a check to the dealership service department for the repairs, which was around six thousand dollars. He drove the rental truck for three weeks and the company billed us for it. We didn't get a check for about two months.

I had started chemo. He got his little social security check in. My insurance rate went from four hundred fifty dollars a month to eight hundred and fifty. They didn't even send a letter. It was group insurance taken out of the settlement checks. I had no choice but to keep it. When all of this was said and done, I owed the cancer center over five thousand dollars and we hadn't had a check in eight weeks. We made it. We absolutely made it and we didn't get hungry and no utilities were shut off.

The cancer center called me in to the finance office. That got me just a little bit. I had no idea what to tell them about when I could start to pay. They had a wonderful solution. I walked out of that office knowing that God had performed another miracle for me.

My story is simple, the doctors didn't write it. God wrote it before I was born. He knows my days, and the hairs on my head. What's a testimony without a test? It is just another step on the road to Glory.

Jan 18, 2013

What a mighty God we serve... Angels bow before Him; Heaven and Earth adore Him... Now, does He want me healed instantly or is there someone watching for my reaction? Here it is. We serve a mighty God and I don't care how He does it or when, so long as He gets the glory. Those who know me know that I cannot do this on my own, but with His help.

I go back to the doctor this afternoon to find out what his final diagnosis is. (Is it fairly new or has it been here for a while) and then he will tell me what treatment plan he has in mind for me. He worked at the Mayo Clinic for 4 years, which really helped me and Awesome Joe to be able to talk to him easier. Thank you, Lord for putting those in my path who will help me and whom I can witness to. I should pray the prayer of Jabez, 'Enlarge my territory, so that I can bless others, and show your Glory all around" 1Chronicles 4:10). He'll be there to help you when you call upon His Name. He can still deliver by His Almighty Power. While here below it's good to know He's still in the fire."

Jan 21, 2013

I have Stage 3, Follicular Non-Hodgkin Lymphoma, Intermediate with tumors up to 4.5 centimeters in my abdomen. PICC line inserted Monday 1/21/13 for Chemo to start (hopefully) tomorrow. Strangest thing, one of the nurse technicians at the hospital was a spirit filled lady. She prayed with me and was amazed at all that is going on.

These doctors did not write my life story. God wrote it in gold and blood before I was ever born. He has my life planned from the time I am born to the time of death, and He knows exactly how many hairs I have on my head. This didn't just HAPPEN. I have cancer for a reason. If I can change the heart and soul of just one person, then Lord, please use me.

Our God is an Awesome God and I plan to Let go and Let God.

Jan 17, 2013

I am so amazed at my friends and family. They have all taken upon themselves to check on me... no negatives (just as

I asked), they tell me I can do this. I think we are still reeling in the shock of the diagnosis, but that seems to be the best part. No one has come in and dropped major bombs on us, it has come in steps. I have time to get used to this fact before I go further. Through it all, I know that God is my Healer and I can't wait to see how He handles this one. As I told my family, 'You can't have a testimony without a test.'

I do know where my strength comes from and I know in whom I trust. I knew a long time ago the FAITH is Fully and Implicitly Trusting Him. (Psalm 23) My next thoughts are, "LET'S GET THIS PARTY STARTED NOW'

I got it.
Jan 25, 2013 4:43pm

Thank you all for your prayers. I got the approval! I start Tuesday morning at 8:45. Now, you may think it silly to be excited about starting chemotherapy, and honestly, I do too. But, I was beginning to think I would have to take the paper work to the insurance people. God's timing is perfect. I just want to get this party over with. Thank you, Lord for teaching me patience even in this.

God wrote my life story
Jan 26, 2013 9:11am

(Jeremiah 1:4-5, NIV), "Before I formed you in the womb, I knew you, before you were born I set you apart; I appointed you as a prophet to the nations."

How can I not believe that God has a purpose for all things, including this? One of my doctors is from India. Is she a Hindu in need of Jesus? I don't know, but I intend to take every chance to talk about His Glory. Does one of the nurses need Him? I don't know. All I know is it is now my job to witness, and to witness I must maintain a happy demeanor and strong front. Today I ask all of you to join me in that prayer. I do not want to fail in this task, because I want to win the race.

I am not stupid and I know that there will be times when I don't feel good, I just ask that you pray I will be able to smile and continue to praise HIM who knew me, and formed me, and trusted me enough to give me this task.

My greatest example of faith was Mrs. Kim Allen. I never saw anybody fight that hard before. I loved her and she left me with a hard job to do. May I just be worthy of the calling. LET GO, LET GOD.

When my daddy was alive, he would turn the music up just as loud as he could get it, and then my phone would ring. He would yell into his end, "Ida, can you hear this song?" They would be playing something like I'LL FLY AWAY or one of those old ones. I would yell back into the phone, "Daddy, what did you say, I can't hear you over the music." It was our game.

When I met my Awesome Joe, he would listen to his favorite singer, Connie Smith, and he would call me on the phone and say, "Can you hear my baby singing to me?" I would answer, "I can't hear you, the music is too loud." He loves to hear her sing How Great Thou Art.

Now, I had a pretty good rendition of my own, but he would never even hear of me singing it. Connie has to sing that one.

Last Sunday, at The Barn Fellowship, our band played How Great Thou Art. I recorded it on my phone, and I called

Awesome Joe later in the day and I said, "You have to hear this." To me, hearing Brother Jerry and the band play and sing that song was the most blessed I have ever heard. So, I said, "Can you hear this, Joe?" His answer was, "You know I can't hear stuff like that. What are you doing anyway?" I think he forgot how to play that game.

What, I can't drive car for today
Jan 27, 2013 9:12am

My husband is my protector and my strong arm that God gave me to love me. When he says you better just take it easy, then what else can I do? I have a friend coming by today to look at the PICC and she may put more protection on it. Not sure. I just know if I were to jerk on the steering wheel with my left arm, it could be bad. For now, Awesome Joe says, "Do not drive." I asked him how I am supposed to pick up Hannah and get to church; he didn't have an answer. Guess I will work on that this week.

On the other hand, I sure do like just relaxing in the living room in my pajamas and listening to music. I have a quiet worship playlist, and I turn the TV on but don't really listen. Just let the music soothe me. God has been good to me, and the music is there, in my computer, all I had to do was create the playlist.

I thank God for a comfortable home and friends and family who have offered so much help in the coming weeks and months.

I was quiet for a day....

Jan 28, 2013 9:06am

Well, I knew I couldn't drive the car, so I just stayed home in my pajamas and rested. I need to be ready for tomorrow, Tuesday, my first day of CHEMO. I will confess to you I am nervous. I have prayed, you are all praying for me, and I know this will work out for God's glory. That being said, I am a big baby and I don't like surprises.

God is good to me, and all of this has come in Baby Steps. This all started almost 4 months ago. End of October when I was in doctor's office for annual blood work and stuff. He told me to get a Mammogram as soon as possible. November is a hard month for me, what with getting ready for the Big Community Thanksgiving Dinner and all. So, I put that off until December 4. I still didn't think anything was wrong.

Around the 15th of December I got a letter from Ross Breast Center, they said the doctor had seen something and was waiting to compare to my last mammogram (which was 3 1/2 years ago). I told Joe I didn't like that. A few days later I got the call and was asked to come down for further studies, which I did on the twentieth.

The doctor there told me I needed 2 biopsies and we scheduled it for the 8th of January, because I was planning to spend Christmas with Joe. But the 8th found me back down there in Tyler.

Over the last few weeks, I've been learning in Baby Steps. Then one day last week, I took a wrong turn and walked right into the Chemo room; my last step. I panicked when I realized where I was and turned and walked out quickly, but then I realized that God had just helped me to prepare for tomorrow morning. I know what to expect when I go in there. Only thing left is to find out how it actually feels; the last step.

And when all is said and done, I have 12 treatments scheduled. They come 2 at a time, Tuesday and Wednesday, every 4 weeks. I can tell you now where I will be. Then he said 2 years of maintenance. Another step, but it can't compare with tomorrow.

I would be lying to you if I didn't say I am nervous. But thankfully, I have God on my side. How does anyone face this without Him? How horribly lonesome that must be. Psalm 91, He that dwelleth in the secret place of the Most High, shall abide in the shadow of the Almighty. I will say of the Lord you are my Refuge, and my Fortress, My God in You will I trust. He will give His angels charge over thee, to keep thee in all thy ways, Psalm 91.

I am not afraid, just a little nervous of new things. But, so long as I can keep Him at the front I will be alright.

On a humorous tone, I saw a video on Facebook this morning and I shared it. First thing you see is a little boy walking a dog. The dog is well trained. There is a puddle in the road, and the little boy deliberately walks through it, then he lays the leash down, very carefully, and goes back and runs in and out of the puddle several times. The dog sat patiently and waited until that little boy came back and picked up the leash to finish the walk. I laughed so hard; it was so funny.

Reminds me of the skunk that got in our neighbors' trash can when I was a kid. The city was called, they came out and shot the skunk in the can and left him, saying they would be there in the afternoon to get rid of him. But it stunk really badly. It was REALLY BAD. My little brother, Clevern, went over (against Mom's orders) and took that skunk out of that can and carried him about a mile from the house down in the creek bed and left him. He had to be treated for the smell, and that was funny. But hilarious was watching two men from the city come with hooks on poles and wiggle around and complain about having to do the job. We tried to tell them the skunk was gone, but they wouldn't listen. Finally, one of the men said that trash can sure was light to have a skunk in it. They argued over who would look. They had been handling that can from 4 feet away on each side, like it was going to bite them. You should have seen their faces when they finally opened the lid and the skunk was gone. HAHAHAHA. My little brother was always good for a laugh. He is too much like my daddy.

Chemo today
Jan 29, 2013 8:07am

I will be inside the hospital in just a few minutes for my first chemo. Thank you all so much for your prayers, love and support.

Praise God from whom all Blessings Flow
Jan 29, 2013 6:03pm

Today was my first chemo. Hallelujah. I am blessed, tee-totally, awesomely wonderfully blessed. I couldn't have done it without your prayers. We had people promising to pray from lots of places, Texas (of course), Arizona, California, Iowa, Illinois, Indiana, Kentucky, Michigan, Wisconsin, Washington, And even from India. I have Senatorial candidates, Baptist churches, Pentecostal churches, Full gospel churches, well known southern gospel musicians, and truck drivers all praying for me today. I know that because I felt the prayers, and I knew that God was in the room with me all day.

I did NOT get nauseated, or faint, or any other adverse reactions. As Leon Pickens (my step-dad) said, all I did was sleep, snore and go to bathroom. Only God could have done that for me. Only your prayers could have caused Him to give His full attention to me today. Thank you for bombarding Heaven for me. Thank You for giving me that kind of attention, you have blessed me this day.

All of this said, I am tired now and in serious need of, you guessed it, more sleep. I just pray that all continues to be well as the meds work their way through my system. I intend to have a long night of sleep. I love you all and I thank you so much for blessing me today.

Good morning
Jan 30, 2013 9:48am

Well, here we go. One more day, and then I can rest for a few days. Today will be a short one. They said it might take an hour. That's probably good, because I didn't sleep well and I look terrible.

The good news is I feel fine; the bad news is you can't see it. I am supposed to stay away from people for the next several weeks. Crowds carry germs, they said, and I can't afford to get close to germs. I didn't think it prudent to tell them I sleep with a Toy Poodle named April. They'd probably drop dead in their shoes.

I think I was just overly excited about how everything went yesterday. I kept trying to go back to sleep and kept getting disturbed by things that usually don't matter at all. The storm will usually help, but not last night. The cat wants in when it storms and in he came. That's another wake up.

So glad it's a beautiful morning. But because it is, April wanted out at daylight. That finally tore it. I got up and stayed up. She, on the other hand, went right back to sleep.

I have my music going and it is wonderful. He rescued me, new life I can see. He reached out in Love, My Jesus reached out in love and He rescued me.

His healing will take me through. I am confident of that. His Grace is sufficient for me, and I will use it to the fullest in the coming months.

Have a great day.

So much for short
Jan 30, 2013 6:47pm

This is funny. The Fed-EX truck never got there with my medicine for today's treatment. The hospital pharmacist had to finally get in her car and go somewhere else to get it for me. My 'short' visit to chemo turned into about 3 hours. All for a little bag of chemicals that takes 30 minutes to run into my body. That will definitely teach me to watch what I am doing. Glad I went prepared with a book and with games on my tablet.

I am back home now and do not have to return to Tyler until next Wednesday for a dressing change, that's once a week, and then I go back to chemo on the 26th of February. Think I will get into my pajamas and pretend I am alone. (Because I really am now). I am tired and ready for bed, and maybe I will sleep all night tonight.

Joe is in Phoenix and will be watching television with a friend until bedtime. I really do thank God for him; he takes such good care of me. And he has friends in places where he seems to get stuck for a few days. I miss him, but he is doing what he does so I can do what I do here.

This is short, but I am tired, and God knows I need some rest. Love you all.

Restful day today
Jan 31, 2013 8:22am

We exclaim our God is Mighty, lift up your name for you are holy, in adoration we bow before your throne.

I have the day off. Yeah. Think I will attack the office/paperwork for an hour or two and stay down the rest. These trips to Tyler simply wear me out. On the other hand, I had a very good night. I did wake up around midnight to April demanding to go out, then the cat snuck in on me. He kept me up for about an hour before my grandson came to my rescue. Have no idea why but he came in and took that cat and put him back outside before doing whatever he came in for. I was out like a light immediately. See, the cat, named Pooh Bear because he was so cute when we got him, looks like Garfield now. If he plants all that weight on you, you can't move, and he thinks he is my appointed foot warmer. If I move he moves, if I take them out from under the cover, he attacks them until I cover them back up. He's crazy.

Otherwise, I had a really good night. I can't remember Corey walking out the door, but I know he did, and he locked the door behind him. I think he probably felt I was in distress. We do have that connection and I was praying for relief. God sent him to help me.

I love to watch the back yard
Feb 1, 2013 9:04am

The birds come in to eat, the sun hits the grass, and the squirrels run around. An occasional rabbit reminds me life goes on. I get to watch stray cats sneak up in the yard, and I get the pleasure of making sure they don't get Pooh Bear's food. The trees are all brown and dead right now, but in a few months, they will be turning green and lovely.

In Ecclesiastes, we are told there is a time and a purpose to everything. This is my time, and I am fulfilling my purpose. He has set a path before me and it is up to me to choose how I will go forward. I choose life and happiness. I choose to glorify the living God, who can, and who will heal me of all my diseases. I refuse to give in.

These doctors can have a lot of crazy ideas, but I promised God I will try to do as I am told (that's not easy for me, because I am hard-headed). Right now, that means I stay home and avoid all chance of attracting germs. PERIOD. I have 2 full weeks of this. Awesome Joe says it means I can't leave the house until I go back to the doctor.

It means I have to drink a gallon of water every day. I'm swimming. And they said only 1 soda pop a day. That's the hardest part. Give me that Diet Pepsi. I am tired of water, but no, I promised. And I am trying to be good. I just can't have the caffeine. And then yesterday they must have added chlorine to the tanks, because this water was awful. But I drank it.

It is better today, and I am drinking it again. They said I have to keep flushing the chemicals through my body. I am trying to be good.

My friends are coming from Phoenix today. They will be here for a few days. She has promised to take good care of me over the weekend. They called Joe and told him they were coming, and he lectured them about coming in here sick. He told them don't even try to come in here if they were sniffling or sneezing. He is really trying to take care of me. I love that man.

Corey and Sandra have made it their personal mission to keep everyone out unless they are vetted first. And then Corey got the sniffles. Now he won't come thru the door. He is taking this literally. God has truly blessed me with a family that cares for me and loves me.

My friend, Marie, who lives right behind me, has been coming to help me in any way she can, including bringing me food. She is great.

I have had offers from so many of you, and I promise you, the time will come I will need to call someone, but right now, I am still standing strong and trying to do all I can for myself. I can't tell you what it means to have all your love around me.

Awesome Joe will be home on Sunday night, for a few days, and there are some things he can do. I just need to see him.

God is so good to me, and I am so blessed to be here at this moment.

The Son is Shining on Me
Feb 2, 2013 8:26am

I look out the window and see where the sunshine is hitting the yard in so many places. Maybe we will have an early spring, not sure, I thought sure it would be a long cold winter. What I do know is that the grass is turning green again and beginning to grow. It reminds me that Seasons change, and life does too.

I have friends here for the next few days. Friends I have needed to see. Members of my family have called a lot, but for one reason or other they can't come. Some are too far away, some are sick with colds, some are simply busy with their own lives. That's okay. I know they all are praying for me and they love me. But this friend who is here today, well, she introduced me to my Awesome Joe and she is like my sister from another mother. She will be able to help me with a few things that I wouldn't let anyone else do anyway.

God is good like that. He knows exactly who we need to do certain things for us. He knows what our limits are. He knows how to stretch our faith and pick us up and say, "It's my turn now." And then for a while in the walk you will only see one set of footprints.

I am certainly thankful to all of you for all that you have done. I feel better now, but still very fatigued. My hip is sore and I don't know if it's because of the chemo or the Fibromyalgia or if I knocked it out of place. I haven't fallen or anything, just not sure. With the location of the Lymphoma, it could be either, or neither. I am praying for relief on that.

Talking to Awesome Joe about the need for a ramp outside, so that my mother can come and visit me, and he says maybe. It's difficult for me because I am used to going out whenever I want to and getting things done.

I do know God has a purpose in all of this... I am waiting on Him.

FAITH IS ....
FULLY
AND
IMPLICITLY
TRUSTING
HIM.

And I do. No matter what happens.
I trust Him with everything.

I am ill today.
Feb 2, 2013 6:07pm

    I am so glad my friends came. Today was the first time I actually took anything for a sick stomach. I have slept off and on all day. I sure am glad we have a big God, because I can't imagine being here without Him. Awesome Joe is still sitting in Los Angeles and won't be home until Monday afternoon.

Another beautiful day
Feb 3, 2013 12:11pm

    Our Heavenly Father knows the hairs on our head, so He knows how much we need sunshine and birds singing. He responds with a sunny day, nice and warm, so we can actually breathe the air.
    It's another step on my journey, but here I am. I am at home, and my friends have gone to get a few things for a "Superbowl Party" that I can participate in. We are all afraid that any spices will upset my apple cart completely, so she said she knows what to do. I bet she does too. She could probably make anything work and never complain about the extra work involved so that I can participate. She told me to rest and allow myself to be spoiled. Okay then.
    Awesome Joe is in Arizona, on his way home, but probably won't make it until Tuesday morning. He didn't get loaded until late last night. Either way, I am secure in his love for me; and I am so blessed to have him in my life.
    I am missing my mom, but she has had a cold and can't get near me, and then we have to figure out the logistics. Either I go there, or she has to climb my steps. I hope she feels better soon, because I would love to hug her.

My son hasn't been able to come, because they can't be sure the virus is eradicated from their home. One day soon, I will look up and he will be here.

We are surviving on phone calls and texts, and that will just have to do. Awesome Joe says I can't play with the GERMS.

Just for today, I will leave all behind and follow Jesus. That's what the song says, "I will follow Jesus". Back in the beginning I asked that He would use me and be present with me at all times. And I am trying to keep myself open to Him. He is my strength and my shield. He is my fortress. He is my strong tower!

Super Bowl
Feb 4, 2013 12:12am

I watched the Super Bowl with my friend from Phoenix. She was pulling for San Francisco, but I told her after the 3rd play the Ravens were going to win. She brought me some snacks and we had our own little party; just enough to enjoy but not enough to get sick on.

God brings people to us as we need them, allows them to stay for a while and then lets them leave again. Sue and Gary will be here until Wednesday, staying just long enough to see Awesome Joe for a few hours and then they will be gone again. He will be here until Friday afternoon late.

This is God's way of letting me have company, without wearing me down. I can see his hand in the mixer, and I love the colors. Dewayne said today they are all feeling much better and he hopes to be able to come soon for a short visit. I really miss them; I'm used to seeing those kids pretty often.

I should be through this complete quarantine soon, and I am making it with His help, but I don't know when the doctor will allow me to get into a crowd again. The chemo is very strong, and they are worried about me fighting off anything.

The man next door to us thinks he has a big ranch. He has 2 acres, I know because Joe sold it, yet he's up to 3 cows, a donkey, 3 sheep and about 2 dozen chickens. Gives my outside dog something to play with, but I am not sure where he puts them at night. Do you think he could just be fertilizing his yard and then planning for a bar-b-cue? That would leave the donkey and he really loves to play with my dog.

Jesus is the Way, Truth, Life
Feb 4, 2013 9:40am

I am so glad I have a Father who loves me, and a Brother who chose to make sure I was brought in by adoption to serve inside His grace, and protection for the rest of my life. I have a song playing that says, "How long, How Long, Till I become Like You?" The answer is up to me.

You see, the more I worship, the more He can take over. It is up to me to Praise my Father, to read and absorb His word, to come to Him in true Worship. And when I become completely enveloped in HIM, then He will envelope Himself in me. It is the purpose for which He sent us here. To become like Him, and to show the world that He is THE WAY, THE TRUTH, THE LIFE, and that WITHOUT HIM there is no other way by which man can come to the Father.

No matter how much we say it, we have to breathe it, live it and be guided by His Spirit. Otherwise, the enemy is waiting to steal our testimony any way he can, and he will. It's hard enough to be human and live a Spirit-filled life; if you stray away from His Word for a while you can fall. It's a constant chain of keeping things going right.

I am supposed to be fighting a battle right now, yet it is not my battle, it belongs to my Father. I believe that Jesus Christ took stripes for my healing before He was crucified. He didn't forget about it. He took every single disease with him. Every single stripe. My healing. Hallelujah.

We had a wedding at church yesterday, a Barn Fellowship wedding. I am so sorry I missed it, but God knows what He is doing with me. Patience has never been my best virtue, and I want Him to hurry up, but it is for my good, so I choose to LET GO, LET GOD.

Feb 5, 2013 10:16am

Yesterday was hard for me, but we have to take the bad with the good. I am lucky to have a few friends who are willing to give me their day and help me so I don't have to do much right now. I am blessed to have friends and family who are calling to check on me and offering to do for me. When you are confined to the house you realize how much you miss just walking out to feed the dog or check the mail.

Awesome Joe is coming home today, and should be here in a few hours. I have missed him so, but he is doing what he has to do for us to survive.

We put God at the head of our household triangle when we married, (Joshua 24:15 KJV) says "As for me and my house we will serve the Lord." That means all the time, not just when we want to. We will serve Him and we will praise Him for all that He is doing for us. I am doing all that I can to be obedient. That means doing what the doctor tells me to, because I didn't hear anything different.

My Oncologist worked at Mayo Clinic for 4 years. I have confidence in his treatment, and seeing that certificate really helped me and Joe to feel more comfortable. You see, this is not a CURABLE cancer. It can be slowed down, it can be treated, but the only way to get rid of it is to be completely HEALED by the stripes on Jesus back. I will take it, but that wasn't what we felt we needed to do. We both felt comfortable and confident with the decision to go to Texas Oncology and work with them. All I can do is pray that God will use this for His Glory and then my life will be a testimony. (You can't have a testimony without a test).

My daddy used to entertain all of us by putting his hands in his pockets and doing a jig. As he danced, he would sing, "Did you ever go a fishin' on a bright sunny day, when all the little fishes were out to play? With your hands in your pockets, and your pockets in your pants, see all the little fishes do the boogie woogie dance." We would all just laugh, and later he would sing it to our children. I guess I am a lot like my daddy, because he wouldn't, couldn't eat meat unless he knew every child on the block was fed. He couldn't stand to see people going hungry. He loved life, loved to laugh, and lived to serve.

I love my mom, but it took me years to realize she wasn't the big bad bully from the neighborhood. She had to hold us down. She had to be the stabilizer in daddy's world. She was the disciplinarian of the family, mainly because daddy worked so much. She never told us to 'Just wait till your father gets home." Nope, she would tell us to go get a switch. And she didn't mean just any switch. She wanted a switch off that weeping willow. They were soft. They would wrap around you and get you good. One time, she told my brother to get her a switch, and he ran. He was running down the street, yelling, "Call the police, she's murdering me." As I remember it, Mom cut her own switch, got in the car, drove right up behind him, and whipped his tail all the way to the car. Then she got him home and gave him another, just for running.

She didn't always whip us, we had lots of wonderful times growing up. We were very poor, but didn't realize it until we were grown. My sister went off to college and wrote a paper about the shack we grew up in and we were all mad at her, until Mom told us she was right. The main thing my parents taught us was love.

We could fight everybody in town, but we couldn't fight each other. Not even as adults. My parents would get right in the middle of us and tell us so. We had to stick together for each other. When my daddy passed, he didn't leave a will. All of our spouses stood back, and said they were waiting for the fight. They got surprised. We didn't have anything to argue or fight about. We love each other and that is all there is to it. We signed every document and daddy's estate was settled within 3 weeks. WE LOVE EACH OTHER. That's my daddy's biggest legacy.

Untitled
Feb 6, 2013 10:24am

Rough day so far. I have gone back to bed and left them to fend for themselves. God will help me rest though, and I will be back up soon. Love to all.

I'm okay after resting

Feb 6, 2013 12:18pm

I slept for about an hour, and woke feeling better. Then, I started getting messages on my phone, and on Facebook. Wow, God wanted to make sure I get back into the race.

Someone wanted the words to a song "Walk on through the night", and just used that to remind me I am not alone. Others wanted just to say, "Hang in there." My friends are totally awesome, and my family is such a blessing.

My baby sister sent me a message two days ago. "Hope you're doing OK. No. Not OK. GREAT, WONDERFUL, STUPENDOUS, GROOVY, RADICAL, FAROUT!!!!!" That meant a lot to me, because Martha lives in Michigan and we can't see each other or talk as much as we want. When she started praying for me just before the Chemo started, she reminded God of every good thing I have ever done for her. I think she must have taken the time to write it down, and then she reminded Him of other good things I have done, that many others wouldn't even try. Finally, she asked My Father to use this time to return those blessings to me. I was crying, and she just kept going. I do love my family, even though we don't see each other much. Like I said before, my daddy's biggest legacy was the love we have for each other.

I have 3 brothers and 3 sisters. My mother used to say she could write a true book about our lives and no one would publish it because they would think it was all made up. There are many tales to tell. 2 of my sisters are saved, and 2 of my brothers. The other 2 need to know Jesus power and I am hoping they will see it through me in the next few months. I want all of them to join me, and I want all of my family to be saved.

My tummy is still a little volatile, so I think this will be all for now. Glory to God in the Highest. He lives, He saves, and He loves me.

Pray my numbers are good
Feb 8, 2013 7:02am

This morning Awesome Joe and I are up early because I have to be at the doctor office in Tyler. They will do lab work, then I see the Nurse Practitioner, and then they change this ugly dressing on my arm, and make it pretty and new again. I have been eating, forcibly, at the hands of everybody here. They cook it and bring it, or just sit and watch me, my proteins and all should be really good. Also, because no one will let my glass run dry, I am drinking about 90 to 100 ounces of water every day. Another requirement, if not they go to extremes with other methods. I don't want other methods. I just want good numbers.

I asked Joe the other day if he could see the blue in my green eyes. He said no, and then wondered why. I said we could all go swimming in the water I have been drinking.

I will let you know later that everything is all right.

Praise God for Good news.
Feb 8, 2013 3:12pm

The ANC (don't ask, because I know less about medicine than I do about what's under the hood of my car) numbers were good and she said my kidney function is good. In fact, both numbers are better than they were the day I started chemo. That's a praise report right there. They told me my first ANC was 2700, if it drops to 1500 they get worried. It was back up to 3300.

I have to say thank you to everyone who has encouraged me to eat, and who has poured me gallons of water to drink. Those of you who kept me at it have had a huge impact on my health. I like it when the numbers get better rather than worse. They said it was normal that I have slept so much the last few weeks.

Now, I go back on Wed, 13th for another dressing change to the PICC line, then I have about 2 weeks where I can actually get out of the house, maybe eat a salad or two, before chemo again on the 26th and 27th. Isn't that exciting?

Joe actually walked into a cafe we love today, and asked them if we could get a table by ourselves so he could bring me inside. He explained that I am having chemo and can't get around people, but that he wanted to feed me before he left on the road. They gave us an entire room all to ourselves and kept others out for the time we were there. The server came in and said, "I am not sickly today, you are in good hands." That just tells me how good God really is.

He cared enough to put Awesome Joe into my life to take care of me at this time. I love that man so much.

Now, I am tired and ready to get back into the pajamas and rest for a while (which probably means a good nap) because I have a life to get back to soon.

CHAPTER FIVE

When all of this started, back in December of 2012, I was really sick. I would get out of bed and move into the living room, and there I sat around in the chair. I was to the point of paying someone to clean my house. My weekly, monthly and annual bookkeeping was stacked in piles on my desk and I had done nothing in months, with the exception of the food ministry.

I had started that work in our home in January of 2011. I went and bought fifty dollars' worth of groceries. My husband came in and I was sorting the bags. I had enough to give two families, the basics for 5 days for a family of three or four (if the children were small). I brought it home, and he came in.

"What's all this?"

"I am not sure. I just felt like we needed to help someone," was my reply.

"What are you doing?" His questions were boundless. "What are you going to do with it, now that you have it?"

I told him I was sorting it so if someone came we could help them. He was astounded at first, but then he decided it was a good idea. "Where are you going to put it, and who is it for?"

"I don't know." I was still trying to get it all bagged separately. "Maybe I will just put it in a box and set it in the corner of the living room."

He jumped on that really fast. He went to his shop and came back with some boxes.

We set the food in the corner of the living room. It was my week to stay home and work on books. He left to do his run to California. Every day he would ask me if anyone had come. I had no idea how to get the word out without having the house overrun with people needing help, so I decided to trust God to bring to me someone who needed help. The next week, I bought another stash of fifty dollars.

After about three weeks, I woke up with a name on my heart. I called my friend and explained that I did not want to embarrass her, but that I couldn't stop thinking about her. I told her I had this food. Within just a few hours, she was at my house. It wasn't for herself. She brought another friend who had seven children at home. She was unable to work and her husband had been laid off of work. They were hungry. I talked to my Awesome Joe and we gave them what we had. We prayed for them and for the food, which needed to be enough to help, and that they would be blessed. Within a few months, I had to buy shelves. I would come home from the store, and there would be boxes of food left on my porch. We converted one of the bedrooms to a storage room. Word spread very quickly and we were helping ten to fifteen families a month within 3 months.

By mid-August, we were helping up to 25 families in a month. People were donating food and my friends and partners would come and sort it out. We were busy. I was now staying home full time to work this ministry. If I got the chance to go out with Joe, then I would have a friend to come in and check my messages. It was really fantastic to see what God was doing. Joe and I had agreed that if this was where God wanted us, then I would do it. I have not been back in the truck but for one week since June 2011.

I AM A VICTIM OF AMAZING GRACE

In late August, 2011, we had a prayer meeting and then discussed the food ministry with several friends. We wanted to do something really big for the community we live in. Our little town has about five hundred people and it is estimated that three fourths of them are on disability or welfare. It is a very depressed area. We decided to prepare and serve Thanksgiving dinner. We talked about it for a few weeks at several other meetings. Finally, we were ready. We wanted to serve Thanksgiving Dinner, on Thanksgiving Day, to the entire community, anyone who would or could come.

We ordered banners, printed up flyers to distribute around town. We rented a building with a big kitchen and large dining area. We prayed about how much to prepare. We cooked 8 turkeys and all the trimmings. It was a huge undertaking. I could never have done this without my partners.

On Thanksgiving morning, I arrived at the building first. It was six in the morning. Slowly the volunteers showed up. People brought in pies and cakes, other vegetables, gravy, and rolls. The youth group at McClendon-Chisolm Baptist Church came to help serve and to do trash and talk to people. Others came. We had couples who just wanted to give their time. At the end of the day, we had served around one hundred people, plus the people who were there. We took turns eating and shared conversations with those who came in. It was an awesome day and we thought a general success, but we had lots of turkey left over. All the meat was frozen. I didn't know what yet, but we all felt like there was a reason.

A few days after Thanksgiving, while I was doing my rounds and talking to people about the food ministry, I found a very depressed area of people. One tiny little community, all in need of help, and the problems they faced were bad.

I took canned goods and meat; we had a freezer full of meat. The McClendon Chisolm Baptist Church youth group had a food drive and stocked our shelves fully just before Christmas. I had a church group that was giving us fresh vegetables and fruits, as they were available, and even a supply of milk for these families. We were now feeding forty to fifty families a month. When I went into this community, they recognized my vehicle. They needed food and help first, and then we were able to witness and to talk to them.

When I drove up there that day, to deliver food, I met the 'manager' of the community. He told me they were a very poor group of people. He said any help we could give them would be awesome. He pointed out a picnic area which was in the middle of the community and told me we could use it any time. A soup ministry was born that day. Every Saturday we would go in at five o'clock and serve soup, cornbread and dessert. We had turkey, and we used it. We also used hamburger, meatballs, smoked sausage, and chicken. One man brought me a hundred pounds of cabbage and fifty pounds of onions. You guessed it, soup.

After about a month we had others coming forward for soup and food. Soon we were preparing and serving food to 150 people on Saturday, and feeding forty families (at least) every month. The demand was so large we had to buy huge stainless-steel pans for cooking. We bought bowls that could be thrown away or lost, and used them. I would tell the people to bring the bowl back and I would refill it. We cooked in my kitchen, boxed it all up and delivered to different homes, and then we went to that community and set up at the picnic table.

One night a young man was there who asked me what church we were affiliated with. I told him we were from several different churches. He said he would not eat with us because he didn't want anyone preaching to him. I told him

I AM A VICTIM OF AMAZING GRACE

to feel free, but that if he wanted to eat it was free with no forced sermon. I promised him that if he wanted to eat, no one would talk about our churches unless we were asked. He ended up going to church a few months later.

This was before I was diagnosed with Follicular Non-Hodgkin's Lymphoma, cancer, and had to start the chemo. I was so tired all the time, and I was in horrible pain. As time went on, I would start the cooking, others would come in and finish and box the food up. Someone would drive my vehicle to deliver the food. My grandson was the one going to market for me to get what was needed.

When I started chemo, we had to tell the people we could not come back. After a few months all the food was gone. It hurt to close that door, but I know now, as I knew then that God will never close a door unless He is ready to open another. I needed time to heal and to recover all my strength. I got someone to come in and help me and we removed the shelves and made the room back into a guestroom. I trust my Father to take care of me, and to continue to provide for the families we had helped during that time.

Some of those same people have come in to help me here. They have come to clean, or they have just prayed. A few even helped me get the food delivered to others. It really is awesome to see what God can do with just a little bit of obedience.

The Food Ministry was a success. We touched lives. We prayed for people. We prayed with people. We were able to talk to others and to show them a possible way out of the poverty they were experiencing. I do not regret it, not at all. But I also do not regret the closing. Life is a cycle, and we had done as God directed in the ministry.

I needed rest and my Father gave it to me. He is always ready to surround us with His Grace and to allow us to rebuild our own bodies when necessary. Again, I am here because I AM A VICTIM OF AMAZING GRACE.

CHAPTER SIX

In 1986, after many miscarriages, I needed to have a hysterectomy. My dad had passed away on October 9, 1986 and around the middle of November I returned to my OB/GYN. He said I had suffered another miscarriage, that my uterus was prolapsed and that I needed surgery. I arranged for the surgery and went home to pray that all was as God would have me to do. I got confirmation in a dream of my dad. He was walking me through heaven, meeting with my grandparents and others who had already passed. He told me everything would be all right, and that I should just have the surgery. He actually told me this surgery would be good and that the next surgery would be the battle.

I also got confirmation from Jesus himself. One night, as I was crying for all the children I would never raise, never even get to hold, I saw him coming to me. He was in a field of roses. Of course, I told Him I could not get to Him because the thorns would tear my flesh. Jesus bade me come to Him. I took the first step and then He was actually holding me. He told me He had removed all the thorns, and that He was holding my babies and keeping them for me.

On December 19, 1986, they took me to surgery and removed the uterus vaginally, no stitches to deal with. Very little pain, and in just a few more days I was up walking. My mom came to my house and we walked the circle of the community I lived in. Within just weeks, my husband and I were up walking around 4 to 5 miles a day. I felt better than I had in a very long time. My dad was right, that surgery was a piece of cake, very easy on the body.

In late April 1990, I started feeling pain in my right side. Finally, on the first of May, I ended up in the emergency room. They could not even examine me because the pain was so very severe. The doctor ordered a shot of Demerol, and told them to do a sonogram immediately. They found a mass. I thought then, and it still hurts me sometimes to think it, that I had a tubal pregnancy. I do not know. What they told us was that they had found a mass the size of a softball inside my pelvic area, not attached to anything. I told my husband to get my pastor on the telephone. We didn't have cell phones at that time, it was land line only, and if he wasn't there, you just had to leave a message. I have a memory of the phone being held to my ear while the nurses worked to prepare me for surgery. My family was all in the room with me, and everyone made a circle around me and listened to him pray. When I woke up in I was in a room. The pain was unbelievable. Nurses were working on me, and with me. They told me to stay in the bed and not even try to sit up without assistance. I was in that hospital for over a week. My blood pressure was extremely low and because it was they wouldn't let me walk without help. Finally, I began to understand, as consciousness returned. The incision on my belly was about 8 inches long, straight up and down from the navel. My blood pressure was 60/30 when they got me into my room.

On the day before they finally released me to go home, a nurse (or something) saw me in the hall, and said something like, "you're still with us." I told her I was about to go home, and she began to tell me what had happened. While I was in recovery, they lost all my vitals. Nothing recorded for about fifteen minutes, and then, just as the doctor returned to the room, I drew a very loud breath.

I was non-respondent for fifteen minutes. She told me they had lost me in recovery, but that before the doctor could get there I came back. I have no memory of this, but I do know that it took months to get back to normal. I was very weak, and subject to any and all infections. They removed the ovaries and Fallopian tubes, but no mass. The mass was completely gone before they got me to surgery. Whatever it was disappeared, because I am, once again, I am a Victim of Amazing Grace.

I would later ask the doctor if he had taken my insides out and played ball with them, he jokingly responded that he didn't play ball, but he did have everything out of place. I am sure he did.

I have so many testimonies and blessings to speak of, God sending food that was on my grocery list when I had no money, healing me when no one could find a problem, even giving me joy instead of mourning when my husband died.

It's not that we have no problems; it's just that we see problems as opportunities to praise the Lord even more.

CHAPTER SEVEN

There are no PROBLEMS, only opportunities to praise the Lord.

In 2002, while renting a room from a friend, and working as a waitress at a local truck stop, I became very ill. I woke up one morning and was so swollen I couldn't get my clothes on. I prayed for relief. My friend was not home at the time, but one of the other boarders was. He tried to help me, but I was in pretty bad shape. I finally got up and drove to a doctor's office. She took one look at me and said, "I have to run tests, but it looks like Lupus to me."

"I don't know what that is, but I don't have it in Jesus Name." They drew blood. She told me she would be able to answer me in a few days. When she finally called, she told me it was Rheumatoid Arthritis. She said it was really advanced. She prescribed VIOXX and told me to try to rest.

I took the Vioxx for a few days and was able to get back to work. Then I started having horrible pain in my right side. Nothing would help, nothing I did made it any better. I went back to the doctor. This time they said Diverticulitis and Colitis. She prescribed the Levaquin and Clindamycin which are normal for such illnesses.

Three days later I returned to work again. I was about 4 hours into my shift when the assistant manager came out to me and said you don't look very good. I told her that I was going to the local emergency room as soon as my shift was over. She sent me away immediately. I called my son and asked them to meet me at the hospital. I had changed into the uniform at their house earlier, and had my comfortable clothing in the car, but I forgot to take it into the hospital. When Libby came in I was already in triage, I asked her to bring my comfortable clothes from the car. Before I could get changed they had called me back and were putting me in a bed. They told me I was staying and they were looking for a room. Apparently, my vital signs were bad enough they could not let me leave the hospital.

I was in that room several days. Dewayne would pick up my gown each day and take it home, where Libby would wash it and they would return it to me. On the Sunday afternoon, I was laying in that bed praying for God to show the doctors what I needed, when I felt a huge darkness envelope me. It was instantaneous, and yet it was complete. Immediately I felt and saw the light around me. It was glorious; the music was so much more perfect than anything I ever heard before. I was moving toward the end of what seemed like a tunnel when I heard my 2-year-old granddaughter call out to me. I turned to see what she wanted and was immediately awake. I really didn't want to come back, if that was a foretaste of what death is then I am ready.

I felt a pressure on my legs, and when I opened my eyes the clean gown was on the foot of my bed. I grabbed the phone and called my son and said, "Come back, I am awake." That's when he told me he had been in the room nearly an hour earlier. He had Destiny with him, and she did call out to me, but he didn't want to wake me up.

It would be three weeks before the truth was known. I had a heart attack. They didn't know because there were no monitors on me. It showed on an EKG that I had prior to surgery for a kidney stone that was found totally by accident. They scolded me for not telling them, but I did not know until they found it. They said it was a really bad one. They told me I should not be alive.

When you are a Victim of Amazing Grace, things like this just seem to happen. I am a victim, thank you, Lord.

Years later, they can still see that heart attack. They can't define or describe it; my heart just shows the scars, permanent reminders of all that God has done for me. But, this last October when I had chest pains and had to be taken to emergency, after they had done their observation and run all the tests, I had to go back a few days later for an Angiogram, a heart catheter. That doctor was amazed. He said my heart was like a brand new, very young heart with no blockages and no plaque build-up. God took care of that, too. He healed me before they could find whatever it was that panicked those doctors looking at all the results of all the tests.

I AM A VICTIM OF AMAZING GRACE.

It's been like that for most of my life. I have had doctors refuse to tell me what they are testing for because they say I start praying and the problem goes away. Just give me a name, its leaving pretty fast.

And, once God has healed you from it, He won't give it back to you. Many times, people try to pick it back up. They refuse to believe in healing or to accept the grace of an all-powerful God, but He has already taken it from you.

When God forgives sin, He forgives it. It is under Jesus blood and He can't ever see it again. Satan does not want us to believe that. He wants to keep us under condemnation, under judgment. There is a bumper sticker that reads, "Not perfect, just forgiven." That is exactly what we are when we have asked for forgiveness of our sins and accepted the grace of love of Jesus Christ into our hearts. Forgiven, under the blood. It isn't there anymore. And since we are all humans and we sin every day, it sure is good to know that His forgiveness is boundless. Freely given. Free.

Full repentance means to stop doing what you used to do, but it doesn't always work that way for a human. Many of us fall backward. Satan wants to tell you, "That's it. You can't even live a full day for Him, what makes you think He will accept you now?" But, if we are faithful to repent, and to turn from those things which are sin, He is faithful to forgive. And He knows how hard it is to live here in the real world. He is always faithful to call us back and to say, "Come home, my child." All He asks of us is a sincere repentance. He will do the changing and the directing if we will only allow Him. That's what Grace does. Amazing Grace: forgiveness, healing, helping and keeping.

There is a scripture in 1Peter that talks about how He keeps us. He keeps me. His Grace enfolds me and protects me and keeps me. He becomes my conscience and my peace. He reminds me and helps me to do the right things, and He pulls me away from things that will destroy my peace. He keeps me. At times I may pull away from the path that He has set for me.

He will only let me go so far before He gently pulls me back, and then He reminds me I am His and He is keeping me. I am human, and therefore I fall again, but, once again, He will keep me and pull me back. He loves me, and He is ever present to forgive me and to keep me in His arms.

I AM A VICTIM OF AMAZING GRACE. I wish that I could make every person who professes to be a Christian understand what it means to be a victim. I wish everyone could just grasp the concept of talking to Him all day long.

I used to meet with a lady to pray about once a week. Every time she would spend hours telling me what she wanted from God, then she would expect to spend more hours praying about it. In my private prayers I asked God how I should respond, especially since I don't believe it takes a lot of repetition and I had a life to live after I left her house. I began to understand that even my thoughts are communication with Him. Every word that I speak aloud goes straight to His ears. Every word that you and I speak in conversation, every thought you allow to take root in you goes straight to His throne. He is faithful to answer if we pray according to His will and His Word.

The very next time I visited with her, we talked for about three hours. I got up to leave and she immediately grabbed my arm, "Aren't you going to pray with me?" It only took me a second to tell her we had been talking for hours, and that God was in the middle of the conversation, therefore He already knew her desires. She thought about that for a few weeks before I went back. She saw the truth in the statement. Only a God who knows your innermost desires can do that.

The truth is that if we abide in the Word, and if we allow the Word to change us into His image, we become a part of His Word and His Word comes to life in us. This will change your life. Adam and Eve were free to walk and talk with God. They were able to look upon His face and to tell Him of their heart's desires. You and I are no different. The more we are a part of the Word, the more the Word lives through us. As the Word lives through us, our lives are transformed into His desires for us. His Word causes transformation in our lives and conformation in our mind. Then, His will becomes the desire of our heart. Once His will has become the desire of your heart, and the Word is alive, then He can perform His will in our lives very easily. The words you speak begin to line up with His Word, and your words and dreams become reality.

Remember this, His Word is alive and well, and it performs that to which it is spoken. You cannot out speak the Word of God. When you have become transformed into His image, then you become a VICTIM OF AMAZING GRACE.

When you understand that He is listening to every single word you say, that He is part of every conversation, then your prayer life will get even stronger. If you believe that He is in every conversation, then your faith will conform to His presence. When your faith is conformed to His presence then you reach a point where nothing, absolutely nothing, is impossible to you. You will find your thoughts being established. Before you can pray about them, things will happen for you.

It's called intimacy. Our pastor, Jerry Truett, says that a relationship with God should be as intimate as, or more so, than your relationship with your spouse. You become an intimate partner with your spouse. You talk about things that belong only to the two of you. Your children and friends are not privileged to hear some things, but your spouse knows you inside out. You should allow yourself to be even more intimate with God.

One of the things I prayed for with my wonderful husband, Awesome Joe, was that I wanted someone I could love the same way I loved Him, and that he would love me as he loves the Lord. When we started planning our wedding, I asked my friend to sing the song, "I can only Imagine" before the service. I asked the minister to explain that we were honoring God, and that we wanted everyone there to understand that we were inviting them to join us in that quest. I was so excited waiting for my cue. My legs were shaking, and my heart was beating so fast. After she sang, and the minister spoke, then my husband joined him, and then I heard the bells announcing my arrival. (My grandsons rang bells and said, "The bride is here, please stand.") I was sinking with anticipation and nerves, I told my son I couldn't do it, and he just pushed me into that room full of people. My groom was waiting for me and his eyes lit up. He locked those eyes on me and watched me walk through that room. We could only see each other.

Imagine how much more I want to see my Father. I want to kneel in front of His throne and lay my head on His knees and just stay there doing His bidding. I want Him to hold me in his arms and tell me He loves me. I want to hear Him say the Words, "Welcome home, dear and faithful servant. You have done well in my service." I want to anoint the feet and hands of Jesus with my tears. I want to kneel before them for a thousand years or more before I even think about turning to greet those who have gone before. I don't want anyone to get in my way. I want to have eyes for Him only; and I want His full attention for those thousand years. Maybe then I will feel eager to see others, but that's what I want when I cross the river. I want to see Jesus. I want to see God. I want the Holy Spirit to be there with us so that my words will be interpreted fully.

I want intimacy with Him. I want to live and wallow in the Amazing Grace that has been left here for us, and I want to crawl right into that pen and drink of the swill that falls through the cracks. I want to be completely covered in Amazing Grace.

If we are going to wallow in something, it may as well be grace,

God's Amazing Grace.

CHAPTER EIGHT

My journals from the time I was in treatment tell the story of trusting God with everything. I didn't cry. I didn't scream. I could not voice any doubt, and I did not. Everything that came out was positive and uplifting, at least to me.

Feeling Stronger Daily
Feb 9, 2013 5:42pm

Today has been a quiet day, but Marie came and visited with me. I didn't take a nap, haven't even really rested a lot today, which means I am getting much stronger all the time. I will not lie, I am tired now, but this is the first time in a month that I haven't laid around all day. I didn't get out, just sat in living room and dining table with her, but still... it's quite an improvement.

Still bound by my promise to stay down for 4 more days, and then I can get out some. I can't wait. Joe is making sure nothing can affect me. He is really trying to protect me. But after Wednesday, then I have until the 26th before I have another treatment. I may not feel like running a race, and I can't afford to run and get really tired, but I am going to get out of here and go visit my mother. I miss her. She has been having arthritis and nerve pain in her back and can't get into my house to come see me. I plan to make this easy. I will go her direction. She has been so worried about me.

I actually have color back in my face and skin, and feel almost good and human again.

That is all for now. Really ready to rest.

Obedience is better than....
Feb 10, 2013 9:24am

This week I have walked a personal journey through understanding the word OBEDIENCE. It's funny; we don't want anyone telling us what to do. We do what we want, when we want, if we want. And we just keep on walking through life.

Some churches teach women to be obsessively obedient to their husband, even when their husband is abusing them. Thankfully, mine does not. In some cultures, the women are lower than dogs and are not allowed to walk by their husbands' sides. Thankfully, that isn't our culture. Different people translate the words differently, and we are all taught different meanings for the word submission. This is what I have learned this week.

Obedience is better than sacrifice. It isn't always easy. It isn't always what we want to do. But, when a miracle is what you need, then you listen to that still small voice within you and do your dead level best to obey.

See, I prayed for a miracle in my body. I didn't want just a small touch, I need a big miracle. The only way I am going to come through this is with a miracle. The only thing my still, small voice said was that I should do everything the doctors said to the fullest of my ability.

Then, I was reminded that my beloved husband, Awesome Joe, is God's gift to me to protect me to his fullest ability and that he is listening to His voice too.

And, this week, I have read over and over. either in posts on Facebook or in my Scripture, and some have even come to me and said, "God answers you through your obedience." and "If you have faith that God will do what you ask, then you should be obedient to what He asks, because if you are not then He has no responsibility to honor your requests.

Even today, I saw where Gloria Copeland wrote, "One step of obedience in faith can alter your life forever." Wow. One step of obedience. I will not call this submission, except of my own heart.

Normally, I push and push, I do everything I think I need to do. I run around checking on the people here in town who use our food services. I drive people where they need to go. I run and run, and then collapse in tiredness and pain. But the doctor told me, in front of Joe, that I would need lots of rest, and that for two weeks I would need to limit all contact with the outside world, because this Chemo destroys my immunity system. Then, my wonderful Joe made telephone calls. He talked to everyone he knew who had dealt with any kind of cancer and chemo. He made himself a checklist. He found out what was important to my health, and what I need to do.

In the past few weeks, he has told friends with colds to stay away. He has told them I can't see them, they just need to call and say hello. If you remember the roses he brought me before I started chemo, he called me to make sure they were out of the house that morning as I left to go for the first treatment. He has double checked my food list and brought me only what is compatible.

Do I want to get out for a while? You bet. I am a very busy person. But in obedience to his direction, which is what my still, small voice said, I have stayed in and rested, very few visitors, few actions, no salad or raw vegetables. I have done everything he and the doctor said, because that is what my still small voice said to do.

I do this in faith, because I really need a miracle. This cancer is not curable. It is treatable, and can go into remission, but once you are diagnosed with Follicular Non-Hodgkin's Lymphoma, you always have it, and they start counting down your days based on the diagnosis and how far it is spread throughout your body. I was diagnosed Stage 3, because the tumors are all over my trunk, (lower abdomen, mid-abdomen, and upper chest) and because of the size of the tumors (some are as large as 2 inches). The doctor says with this chemo I have a 78 % chance of living 5 years. I REALLY NEED A MIRACLE.

The doctors did not write my life story, God did. Jeremiah 29:11 says He knows the plans He has for me. He knows the hairs on my head.

Awesome Joe says I don't show any fear, he says some people don't understand how bad it really is, because I have not changed my attitude. So, he told me I need to put it in writing. Here it is. I am, once again, walking in obedience. Not because I want anybody crying for me, or feeling sorry for me, but because you really need to know how badly I need this miracle.

I AM PRAYING, JOE IS PRAYING, MY FAMILY IS PRAYING, MY PASTOR IS PRAYING. NOT FOR MY HEALTH DURING THIS TIME, BUT FOR COMPLETE HEALING. I WANT THIS LYMPHOMA COMPLETELY ERADICATED FROM MY BODY. I CAN TAKE NO LESS. Nevertheless, this is God's story and He began it and He will finish it. Either way, we will give Him the praise and Honor and Glory. Forever.

So now you know, this is what obedience is, and why it is so important to me. I REALLY NEED A MIRACLE. May He honor my obedience with healing.

Bad days, Good days, better days
By Ida Helton — Feb 11, 2013 3:50pm

Yesterday was very hard. I had migraine and chemo reactions together. Actually, the worst day I have had. Thankfully my friend, Marie, who has designated herself my caregiver, is a prayer warrior. When I called she came, and immediately began to pray for me. Between her and Corey, I was not left alone for the rest of the day or night. This morning I called and got in to see the chiropractic and he has helped me. He told me there are probably no migraine medicines I can take because they thin the blood, and all of that is on my "Do Not Take" list. He said I should come home and take pain pill and Flexeril and stay in bed rest of day. Chiropractic doctors never like to give pain pills, but it's all I can do.

I am resting now, off to sleep in 30 minutes or so, if the medicines work as they should.

I thank God for all my friends and family who are there for me, but for yesterday I am very thankful for Corey and Marie. Love you all.

Today is to be Great
Feb 12, 2013 8:15am

I declare with all the faith I have that today is going to be great, wonderful, and absolutely outstanding. I missed 2 days of my life to that migraine and side effects. That's enough. I am on my feet, and I am ready to kick some butt.

That enemy better not mess with me today. I am not in the mood, My Redeemer Lives so that I can walk through this with my head up. He lives, so I don't have to be enslaved by all this garbage. I am not giving up because of one bad day. The devil is a LIAR and I have had enough. I am strong today because MY REDEEMER LIVES. I refuse to believe otherwise. And today, I declare, My Redeemer Lives, and I am not afraid of the truth, because the truth is He has set me free.

I can be free from this Lymphoma and I declare it has no hold on me. Just like I said in the beginning, I don't want people crying over me, I want you in agreement with me and praying with me for complete healing. The very next time they start doing tests, I want them to be totally amazed by what they DON'T find.

The chiropractor told me yesterday, he could not find any swollen glands in my neck. That was his first step. It hasn't gotten up there yet. Praise God, it's going to start going away.

Now, my daddy used to have these migraines. My mother only has his reaction to go by. I know that one night it was so bad he rammed his head through the bedroom wall, trying to find some ease. Strange that I should take that from him, along with his compassion for others, I took his migraines. I love my daddy, but he can take this back anytime he wants.

The only thing I want today, and hard to get, is to stand under hot running water for about 30 minutes and get the rest of the kinks out, that or crawl into my spa tub and let the jets and Epsom salt do it. Neither of those is an option because I can't get the PICC line wet, so guess I will make do with a quick shower, with the arm wrapped, and try not to get it wet. Even wrapped, it is pretty difficult because of where it is. But I keep trying.

When we were little, we had one brother who would go out and fight all our battles. Mom always had to chase Clevern down because if anyone picked on any of us, Clevern was going to fight the battle. He was a fighter and he was stubborn, and he was NOT going to let anyone pick on us. I remember one of the other boys came home one day, a little bruised because some bigger boys had beaten on him. Clevern was the smallest one, he got on his bike and went and found the fight. And when he came back his head was (as the poet said) bloody but unbowed. Actually, he had very few marks on him. He showed those big boys who was the boss.

Now, as funny as that sounds, we all grow up and learn to fight differently. I sure am glad that Clevern and his wife, JoAnn, are in a strong church in Kentucky. They are serving God and he takes my prayer to the Master daily. His son, Clevern, whom you see in comments here, is a youth pastor here in Texas and he also is fighting for me. Isn't that wonderful? They are still fighting for me, and it's been 50 plus years. I love you all, Clevern, JoAnn, Clevern, And Kayce. Keep it up, guys, you are making a difference.

Headed to Tyler again
Feb 13, 2013 8:07am

I am going to Tyler again this morning, but it's only for a dressing change, and this should be the last trip until 26th. Marie will be changing them when needed. She has been wonderful to me and I know God put her here for this time.

I feel much better and should have a few weeks of this before the next chemo. I sure am glad the chemo doesn't come more often; don't know if I could handle much more of the huge impact on my body. Need these few days to get back on my feet for a day or two.

I will be going to church Sunday. Hallelujah. May have to cover my face, but don't care. I need church.

Going to go see my mom and I need to see her too. She had a cold, and then she can't get up my steps right now, so I am going to see her as soon as possible.

Glorious Sunshine
Feb 14, 2013 9:53am

I slept late this morning, just didn't feel like getting up. Slept hard, but didn't go to sleep until almost one this morning. So much for taking an afternoon nap when I get home from Tyler. Now, I have missed two hours or so of this gorgeous day. I hate that.

When God gives us days like this, we should be able to enjoy them. We should be able to enjoy the sunshine and the green grass and all that comes with it. The birds singing, the squirrels are looking for a little bit of food. I missed it. But that's okay. I have many days to enjoy.

Yesterday was my last day to drive all the way to Tyler just so they could change the dressing on my PICC line. It has healed nicely and they are going to allow my friend, Marie, to do it. Said I could buy the kits at the pharmacy. $15.00 per kit and it probably costs every bit of that to drive to Tyler, not to mention all the time and how tired it makes me. Not sure how that will change my schedule, but do know that my next appointment is the 26th, 27th for laboratory, doctor, chemo. That means we have a couple weeks to rest up and be ready again.

I also made my first foray out into Wal-Mart, but couldn't get close to the Valentine cards. Wanted to get one for Joe, but people were packed around it like cattle being fed. I stayed far away from that crowd, just picked up what I needed for April, and Lady Blue (the parakeet). Thankfully, those aisles were pretty clear. I'm still not taking too many chances.

I will make a card for my Honey, and maybe I can make it right. He is God's greatest blessing to me and I want him to know it.

I can't wait for Sunday. I haven't been to church in 3 weeks. I need some fellowship. All this SOUL food I get here is not meeting the need. I love my church family and I miss them and I want to spend time with them. I get 2 Sundays, and then another round of Chemo will keep me home for 2 more weeks. That's okay, I am not complaining. God is using this time to heal my body and make me whole again. That's what counts. My obedience to Him, to the doctors, and to my husband will be what allows HIM to work a complete work in me, and HE will do it EXCEEDINGLY, ABUNDANTLY, ABOVE ALL I COULD EVER ASK OR THINK (Ephesians 3:20 NKJV). For that I give Him praise and through all of this He will be glorified.

Happy Valentine's Day. Whatever you do for others, do it with Christ's love.

My new do....
Feb 15, 2013 2:52pm

Well, I ventured out today for the first time. I drove myself to Canton, got my haircut, by the bank, and then the post office. I came back exhausted, but I conquered the drive. I had to pray first, because I was almost afraid to just drive the vehicle. That makes no sense. For me to be afraid to drive is like someone else being afraid to use a pistol (I already don't do that so it wouldn't matter). For me, driving is a way of life, and yet I was afraid of how my body would respond being in the car. So silly. Other than being tired, and ready for a long afternoon nap, I am fine.

Funny, the mailbox in town was full of mail, and the bills are beginning to come in from all over for the biopsy and this treatment. Not bothering me, I just stacked them all up and said, "God, this is your problem." I will have to open them soon, but not today.

My new hairdo is short and sassy, just enough for me to manage without problems, not short enough to be gone. Of course, Lisa, my beautician, understood that I can't perm or color, so she knew exactly what to do. Thank you, Lisa.

My sister and I talked (the one in Michigan) and she is so encouraging about all this right now. She has her faith tied on really tight and that's exactly what I need. She is visiting with her daughter and family in Indiana and was so happy today, because she has her little grandson with her. We prayed so hard for that child to come along, he is a miracle and an answer to prayer. They bought her an iPad for her birthday and she was trying to learn how to use it. It won't take her long. She is self-taught on everything and very smart. I love you, Martha.

Now, something funny happened on the way to ... raising my son. He was about 4 years old, and my mom and I were getting ready for church. I told him several times to bring me the comb so I could fix his hair. He just ignored me. After about 5 times, and probably 20 minutes, and we were late getting in the car now, I said to him rather loudly, "Why do you do this to me? Get that comb in here right now, before I bust your butt."

He left the room and came right back with his comb, grinning from ear to ear, and he said, "I just like to see how long it takes you to get mad."

How's that for a loving son? I almost spanked him, but then I had to start laughing and try not to let him see it.

And now "To Him who is able to do exceedingly, abundantly, above all we can ask or think, according to the power that works in us, To Him be glory in the church by Christ Jesus to all generations, forever and ever, Amen" (Ephesians 3:20:21 NKJV).

Hallelujah. I can't even think of all that God can and will do for me. Amen

---

I Love the Lord
Feb 16, 2013 10:19am

Happy Saturday everybody.

I LOVE THE LORD, and I'LL HASTEN TO HIS THRONE. He heard my cry. I have never heard a prettier song than this one sung by Whitney Houston. What a beautiful talent. And she believed it when she sang it. Whitney's problem was a demon that was bigger than she was. The problem is we don't know how to turn our demons over to HIM. I really do Love the Lord. I try to remember when I hear that song, that it is important to give Him control, and to allow Him to become larger than our demons.

Jesus is the light of the world. It is up to us to show that to the world around us. I am so happy inside myself that He has given me strength to stand and to profess His promises. I don't have to worry about anything else. John 1 says that Jesus was the Light, sent to destroy the darkness man lived in. We must choose which we will do. Live with your demons on display, or show that He is the light of your world.

I refuse to bow down to this problem. I refuse to feel sorry for myself. If Jesus is the Light of the World, and if I love Him as I say I do, then my calling here is to show it to everyone I meet, and to demonstrate that light. I want others to know Him.

I find that I am sleeping at night for about 12 hours, but that I am no longer sleeping ALL day long. I think that so long as I give my body the rest it demands of me, I am doing the right thing. I can't over stress about anything, and I am not going to push myself. Since that fatigue is my biggest problem I will deal with it and allow God to heal my body His way.

All of this being said, I had started on the project of getting my tax work ready for the accountant before all of this mess started, and today I think I will give myself a few hours of HARD LABOR. Shouldn't take more than a few weeks to get all of it done, because I had already done quite a bit, but I pray God will continue to give me strength to do it. I am so far behind.

That means today is going to be a quiet day at home. If you don't hear from me, that's why. I can't do the book work and talk on computer.

God is still in the fire, and He's walking in the flame, He can still deliver by His almighty power. Don't forget. He's worth talking to.

Love you all.

IT'S SUNDAY
Feb 17, 2013 8:44am

CHURCH time and I am so excited. I feel like a kid that just found out he's going to Six Flags today. Of all the things I love to do, church is at the top. I am ready 45 minutes early. You will hear from me later today.

I received this Gift today
Feb 17, 2013 12:55pm

CANCER IS SO LIMITED...
It cannot cripple love.
It cannot shatter hope.
It cannot corrode faith.
It cannot destroy peace.
It cannot kill friendships.
It cannot silence courage.
It cannot invade the soul.
It cannot steal eternal life.
It cannot conquer the Spirit.
It cannot suppress memories.

My pastor gave me this precious gift today. He posted it in the bulletin, knowing I would be there to hear it.

What a wonderful gift to give me. The doctors have told me what this cancer can do; he took it upon himself to tell me what it cannot do. I am so loved and blessed. And the only thing I can add right now is that cancer cannot do anything to me that God does not allow. When Jesus was being beaten for our healing, He knew that at this time there would be a diagnosis of Follicular Non-Hodgkin's Lymphoma, and He put it in the list of diseases that He healed us from. Thank you, Brother Jerry Truett. I love you and Patricia.

Sometimes a diamond
Feb 18, 2013 5:06pm

Well, Corey and Sandra went for my groceries. Awesome Joe has been napping on and off in the recliner. I went back to bed for a while after breakfast. I'm just kind of feeling rundown today. Nothing I could put my finger on. I thank my God for you constantly because I know you are all there for me. I love you all.

Just in case you missed it...
Feb 19, 2013 11:08am

One of my friends posted a video on Facebook this morning and I shared it on my site. It was cancer patients dancing to "What doesn't kill us makes us stronger." How much inspiration can you get?

I was listening to Nicole Mullin sing Redeemer. I know my Redeemer lives. He lives forever I'll proclaim.

That song says, "Who taught the sun where to shine in the morning? And Who told the moon you can only go so far?" Well, it is He, the same God who tells this cancer exactly what it cannot do to my body. Hallelujah.

I remain in submission, I continue to push forward. And even when I have a slow or bad day, I come back fighting. I still have that sign on my wall that says, "YOU ARE GOING TO WANT TO GIVE UP... DON'T"

And then I see the one that has Ephesians 3:20 on it "To Him who is able to do exceedingly, abundantly above all we can ask or think." I can't even think how far God will go to heal me. I can't even begin to think of how good He can be.

I am so blessed.

My Awesome Joe came in Sunday night, and I felt bad yesterday, but today he has offered me a chance to get out of the house for a while. I can't wait to spend a few hours with him. I love that man so much. And our time together is so limited.

Be blessed today, and ask Jesus who you can share Him with.

Our Help Comes From You
Feb 20, 2013 11:45am

Our help comes from you, Lord. We lift up our eyes to where our help comes from. There is a lifting of our hearts, our hands in surrender to you, Jesus.

I am nothing without Him. I love that song that says, "I can't even walk without you holding my hand," because I literally cannot walk without HIM. I can't look around me and see the wonder without seeing Him and knowing that He is there.

We started getting the bills in for the Chemo. I am not shocked at how much they are, because I knew it was ridiculous, but I am shocked at how much of it is left for us to pay. I have to trust that God has a plan for me, and that He is in charge of this. I filed for disability several months ago, and as soon as that comes in they will have to put me on Medicaid or something to help. Please help me to pray about this. I am going to lose my insurance in April anyway; I cannot extend it past there.

One of the medicines they gave me on the 29th of Jan was $10,000. Of course, the insurance adjusts it and then you are left with deductible, but... wow... the deductible wasn't very good.

Anyway, that being said today is going to be quiet. I didn't sleep good last night, and that means I will doze a lot today. April wanted out at midnight, straight up, and then we had the crawl under the covers, and the coming back out... She just wasn't very comfortable. She went back out early this morning, and seems better today. Or I think she is, she's sleeping anyway. Oh, for a dog's life.

Thank you, Clevern for you your prayers, I know God is listening. And thank you Miss Vivian Hale for helping me and supporting me.

God's Grace is Sufficient
Feb 21, 2013 1:36pm

My Grace is sufficient for you, because my strength is made perfect in weakness.

2 Corinthians 12:9

Amazing Grace how sweet the sound that saved a wretch like me.

Amazing Grace is the sweetest song I know.

When I begin to fall I can always reach up and hold on to His hands. He has never, NEVER failed me yet. He always catches me, and on this journey, I have felt him carrying me. Not catching me. He carries me. He holds me in His arms. It's almost like He took all the thorns out of the rose garden so I can just rest and enjoy His presence.

How's that for a thought? An entire rose garden to enjoy without thorns or care. I can deal with that. And sometimes I feel that He has simply placed me in the center (knowing how much I love the roses) and is allowing me to do nothing but rest. Yes, He loves me that much.

Roses can be thorny and hurtful, because you must enjoy the pain to get to the beauty. But for me, He has removed the thorns for now. I am so very blessed.

I want to tell you, Miss Vivian that I know how hard this must be for you, and how it opens the heart to all that has gone before. I pray that God will help you because you have been such a blessing to me. I love you so much for that.

I have chemo again on Tuesday morning, and then I can get back to sleeping for a few days. No, seriously, I have been so nicely taken care of and the rest has been good for me. My family and friends have been on call to me and when I have needed someone they have been here

for me, but thankfully I am able to just rest most of the time. This is so much better than many people told me it would be. That is because
JESUS CAN DO EXCEEDINGLY, ABUNDANTLY ABOVE ALL THAT WE ASK OR THINK.... THAT'S WHAT MY GOD CAN DO (Ephesians 3:20 NKJV).

God is in Control
Feb 22, 2013 10:32am

God is in Control, we believe that His people cannot be shaken. There is no power above or below Him; we know God is in control.

It's an old song, but it works. He is in control. He must be in control, because when we try to control things we mess up big time. We must back off and let God take full control of our lives. It is the only way. He knows His plan, and when we allow Him to be in control, when we wake every morning and make a conscious decision to allow Him to be in charge of the day, we can relax and move through the day without complications.

There is an Orange Juice commercial going around now where the woman meets all the obstacles of her day (car accident, daughter in trouble at school, elevator stuck at work, etc.) and she says "It's a good thing I had my orange juice." Imagine what would happen if you could actually see all those things and say, "Good thing I had my Jesus time this morning."

I could say, "Let go, Let God." or "Remember, nothing is going to happen today that Jesus and I cannot handle together." But if you start your day with Him and then take Him everywhere you go, well, you can't go wrong.

"Take the name of Jesus with you, take it everywhere you go. It will joy and comfort give you. Take it then where ever you go." Isn't it good to know that God is in control and you can cast all your care upon Him for He cares for you, Peter 5:7

I am going to venture out for a bit today, need to go to Wal-Mart and bank and check the mail. That should be enough for one day, and I will come back home and catch up on my day. But I am not getting in that pickup without Jesus, so you better watch out for me. I am not piloting my vehicle.

Funny thing, my oldest sister was about 8 or 9 when she was giving Daddy directions to someone's house. I remember we were all laughing and talking, and she was pointing out, "turn here" or "turn left here". Daddy would laugh and he would say, "you sure?" Of course, she knew where we were going, so eventually the last turn came up. She got pretty excited and said, "Turn right here, Daddy." He did. He turned that old car right into the ditch. The drive was still a quarter mile ahead. (He didn't hurt anything; he was going way too slow for that). When he stopped the car, Edna said, "Why did you do that, you know where the drive is?" Daddy laughed, as only daddy could, and replied, "You said 'turn RIGHT here'. So, I did." My daddy had such a good sense of humor. I wish every child could be as happy as we were.

Be blessed and have a great day.

My Family Cares and Supports
Feb 23, 2013 10:05am

Yesterday I had to venture out of the house for two items which were much needed and to check the mail. I was supposed to go to the bank, but completely forgot about that after I got so tired. So, I came home and checked the box here at the house. Inside was a package from Cafe Press. At first, I was confused, but then I knew what it was. Cafe Press makes t-shirts, hoodies and the like.

I told my sister around the first chemo treatment, that I would love to have the t-shirt that says I CAN FIGHT CANCER, and that there was a hoodie there too. She called my other siblings, I don't know how many of them put in, but she got me the t-shirt and hoodie from Texas Oncology. When I return to the chemo department on Tuesday I intend to be wearing my t-shirt and hoodie. Of course, I will have to take the hoodie off for treatment, but I don't care. It tells me I have the power of the Pickens/McBride clan behind me. When you add that to the blood of Jesus and to His Name, I stand out as a winner every time.

Let me say, I love you all so much. Edna, Pearley, Albert, Alfred, Clevern Sr, Martha, Debby, Kimmy, Kelly, Gail, Kathy, JoAnn, Joe L, Bryan. I think I got all of them and their better halves, I hope so, otherwise please forgive me. I also have nieces and nephews all over this country who are praying for me, my son and his family, and my mother and Leon. How I love them all.

God has blessed me with a wonderful church family at the Barn Fellowship, and I am also very connected to Brookside Baptist. Two complete church families, plus all those of my brothers and sisters and friends. I am really very blessed.

I am way too blessed to be stressed over this little problem in my Lymph nodes, because I know that God is in complete control. Thank you all for allowing me to thank my family today.

Bedtime
Feb 23, 2013 9:51pm

My day was busy in a good way. I spoke to Pearley and Clevern Senior and Joann, Alfred and Kathy and of course to Mom and Pop, and Awesome Joe. I am way beyond tired. Have to be up early for church. Have a good night, and always remember you get out of your brain what you put in. Don't trash it.

Ephesians 6:10-20
Feb 24, 2013 12:52pm

We all know how important it is to keep our hearts ready, to study God's Word, to pray daily. Today, my last day at church for a few weeks because of the chemo, Brother Jerry brought this home to me in a new way.

When I got this diagnosis, I told the devil to stand down in Jesus Name, and I marched forward without fear, without tears. As we read the Word today, and as he brought forth the message, I know how I was able to do that. Verse 10 says, "be strong in the Lord and in His mighty power. Put on the full armor of God so that you can take your stand against the devil's schemes. (v 12) Our struggle is not against flesh and blood, but against the rulers, against the authorities and the powers of darkness and against the spiritual forces of evil in the heavenly realm, (13) Therefore put on the WHOLE ARMOR of GOD, so that when the day of evil comes, you may be able to stand your ground, and after you after you have done everything to stand. (14) Stand firm then, with the belt of truth buckled around your waist, with the breastplate of righteousness in place (15) and with your feet fitted with the readiness that comes from the Gospel of peace. (16) In addition to all this, take up the shield of faith, with which you can extinguish all the flaming arrows of the evil one. (19) Pray also for me, that whenever I open my mouth, words may be given me so that I will fearlessly make known the mystery of the gospel, for which I am an ambassador in chains. Pray that I may declare it fearlessly, as I should" (Ephesians 6:10-19 NIV).

Some of my family and friends, and some of you have asked how I can do this. I guess I was ready for whatever came at that time. I had on the full armor, not just a kneepad. I didn't take my helmet off before I went in to the doctor's office. Brother Jerry said it, and I could see that here I am. I am not saying this to brag on myself, merely to explain that this is where I stand. I had a choice to make. I could fall apart and cry and scream and say why me, or I could tell the devil he is a liar, and I could continue to give God honor and praise. I believe He knew exactly what battles I would face, therefore I must declare that HE is in control, and I will not be shaken.

Thank you, Bro Jerry, for one more time confirming to me that I am doing the right thing at this time. I love you.

When we baptized Tracy this morning, I don't think there were any dry eyes left. I am so blessed to be a part of this congregation. I love you all.

You are Holy, Lord
Feb 25, 2013 12:11pm

Only You are Holy, Lord. You are my Daily Bread. It is your very Word spoken to me. I am desperate for you. You are the Air I breathe. You are my countenance, the lifter of my hands. Help me to remember when the world is crashing that you are my Glory and the lifter of my head.

Help me to steal away. Help me to remember that (just like all the other Christians) I haven't got long to stay here. Your Word says a year is as a day... Help me, Lord, to keep my eyes on You at all times.

I am so awestruck at being in His presence. We are told to be ever ready, in season and out, to give an answer of our faith... I have mine. I am still praying daily that my life will be a testimony to someone in need, that others who see me will want to know this Lord from whence cometh my help. I want to be a living, walking, talking, testimony. I am not afraid to say it is because of HIM that I can do as I do.

My nephew spent the last three months at home with his son, Brayden, because he injured his knee and after the surgery was unable to go back to work. He was in the middle of changing jobs, when he injured the knee, and when he told them he couldn't put any weight on the knee for 6 weeks, they changed their minds about hiring him. He has stood in faith; he has encouraged all those around him. And he prays the best prayers for me. He went to work this morning, kind of, a test of his abilities before they actually put him to work. I love that young man, Clevern, but this picture (posted on my journal) is Brayden and my granddaughter, Destiny. They were having some real fun. Thanks, Clevern, and my prayers are with you today.

Today is the day
Feb 26, 2013 10:04am

This is the day the Lord has made. I will rejoice and be glad in it. Labs done, doctor visited, waiting to start chemo now. I should be called in the next few minutes. Keep praying for a good day.

Headed to the house
Feb 26, 2013 3:41pm

Everything went fine. Once again, God has blessed me with a very good day.

I WILL TRUST IN YOU
Feb 27, 2013 9:11am

Holy, Holy, Holy Lord God Almighty, I will trust in You. You are my hiding place. Whenever I am weak you make me strong, when I am afraid, you bring me peace. I will trust in You.

It's very funny, but the doctor said I should not have slept all that time during the first 2 weeks after the first treatment. I laughed and said, you have no idea how tired I really was. He still wasn't' happy. I said, "You don't understand, my sleep doctor told me years ago I am a Narcoleptic, Insomniac with Sleep Apnea." He says, 'you wear a mask to sleep at night?' Yes. "Oh well, then I guess we're right on track.' My sleep habits have only in the last week returned to normal, I am anxious to see what happens now with the second round of Chemo.

Awesome Joe thought it was perfectly normal for me to sleep 18 to 20 hours a day the first 2 weeks. He knows me very well. And besides, he wouldn't let me do anything else, remember? He tied me to the house and wouldn't let me do anything. (It was because he loves me, but still he knows that is going to put me out.)

Unfortunately, last night I did the same thing I did the first time and slept in 1 to 2-hour shifts. His leaving to go to work at 3:15 didn't help that much. But he doesn't know how long it took me to go to sleep, or how much sleep I actually got. That's the insomnia. I was rather enjoying those nights when you go to bed at 10 or 10:30 and wake at 7, totally refreshed.

Anyway, I sure am glad God gave my Awesome Joe to me for this time. He is doing so well. He really does care for me, and he understands what I need and how to give it to me. (The man can't do laundry or load the dishwasher, but hey, what man can?)

Rain down from Heaven fresh living waters, Come Holy Spirit, bring us your liberty. I have had the song by Nicole Mullin ringing in my ears all night. I know my Redeemer lives. Hallelujah, I know He is working for my good, because His Word says He will withhold no good thing from me.

I wanted to share with you something that happened there yesterday, a lady came in for chemo, but had some tests run first. They called her from the Chemo waiting area and she went back to talk to the doctor for a few minutes. When she came back, she was ecstatic. She got to cancel her appointment for Chemo, and make an appointment with the doctor again in 3 weeks. When they asked her why she was cancelling the chemo appointment, she said, "They just told me I am in complete remission." Thank you, Lord. Her tumors were still there but dead and not producing anything into her body. They will monitor her, but she is done. AMEN.

While back in the Chemo Gallery, as they call it, I heard one of the nurses tell a patient's mother, "There are no nurses in this department who do not believe in God, we have seen too much not to." I am in the right place. Thank you, Jesus.

When I got home, there was my Awesome Joe waiting patiently for me. I love him so much. I'm so happy to be with him for a few hours. This time he should get to come straight back to Dallas, and then we will be all right. Get a day or two together.

Another one done.
Feb 27, 2013 3:00pm

    I am on my way home from Chemo, feeling fine. Praise God.
    Put Brandy on your list, early 20's. She's fighting cancer. She said please pray for her.

I'll be Satisfied
Feb 28, 2013 1:00pm

    When my soul is resting in the presence of the Lord, then and only then am I satisfied.
    What a glorious day. This sunshine has my parakeet (Lady Blue) singing and loving all that she can see. April has played outside most of the morning. Even I feel so much better.
    Last month, when I had the first Chemo treatment, I came home and slept for 2 weeks, 18-20 hours a day. What a difference a month can make. I came home yesterday and swept the kitchen, started laundry. I got up this morning and managed to get 2 more loads of laundry and vacuumed the living room, and am trying to get around to mopping the floor I swept yesterday. This house has piled up since I started Chemo.
    Doctor told me I have to try to be more active, and I just laughed at him. That Chemo hit me really hard. This time, I am much better. My home will look better to me soon.
    I want to say how much I love all of you and all that you have offered to do for me. I had 3 people lined up to help me, and they have and will continue to do

so, but I kept saying I wish someone would just sweep my kitchen and vacuum my living room. You shouldn't offer help unless you are going to do something. But it's okay because I am getting it done now. This makes me remember when my mother had her Hysterectomy after she had nearly died from hemorrhaging in 1962.

The doctors told my mother her surgery was so radical that she was to do absolutely NOTHING for 6 months. It was over a year before she began to get her strength back. We moved from Farmers Branch to Wilmer. Mom had 7 children, and the oldest was barely 11 years old. The biggest church in town sent their welcoming committee to our house. Mom could do nothing, and my sisters and I were all trying to go to school and keep chores done. Those women put their noses in the air and said to my mother that she needed to get up and use a broom on the floor. Then they left my mother in tears, after she had told them her predicament.

We had a neighbor, Mrs. Boren, who had 7 of her own, and she came later in the day to check on us. Mom was in tears telling how those women had treated her. Mrs. Boren laughed her jolly laugh and told my mother next time someone says that to you, you hand them a broom. She helped us a lot back then. We've all lost touch over the years, we moved from that house in 1969. But I have never forgotten the Boren family and the laughs we had together.

I feel tired today but otherwise I seem to be fine. Maybe I will have time for a nap this afternoon. Not a bad report the day after 2 full days of Chemo. I believe the Lord is healing me from the inside out. How about that?

Have a blessed day and be happy.

Old Hymns are the Best
Mar 1, 2013 10:11am

Sometimes I wake up with a song ringing through my mind, today's was "Well, I'm feeling mighty fine, I've got Heaven on my mind. Don't you know I want to go, where the field and honey grow?"

Unfortunately, I do not actually feel so very well, I had a rather rough night, and was supposed to go out this morning on some important business, but decided it is not wise to actually leave the house. Therefore, I am staying home. That's okay. It's probably God's way of keeping me at my resting point until I am healed. I may have done too much yesterday.

Anyway, today I am going to stick to the original plan and stay in the house and rest. I am after all in the first two weeks of Chemo treatment and can't expose myself to a lot of other stuff. The business that was there, Awesome Joe will need to attend to when he comes home. That'll teach him to start giving me work to do.

April, my toy poodle, is actually a little upset with me. I sleep on my left side most of the time and have taken to putting a small pillow there so as to protect the PICC line in my arm. She wants to cuddle up to me, but the pillow is stopping her. I wake up and she is completely under the covers and down at my hip. Then if I move, it wakes her; she has to shake herself off, and then comes out and looks at me, before barreling back under. I know animals can see in the dark, I just wonder what she is thinking when she looks at me like that.

Please pray for Brandi. Brandi is about 20 years old, and was in the Chemo lab with me Wednesday. She has already lost all of her hair, but has quite a spirit about her. I asked her if we could add her to our prayer list and she said please do. I do not know what kind of cancer she has, I only know that God is bigger, and at the Name of Jesus every disease must GO. Thank you.

I love you all. Have a blessed day. Please sign my guest book, so I can see you have been here. I get so excited when the numbers climb. We are getting a bulletin board to hang for the cards I have received. These things mean so much to me. Thanks.

One thing I ask
Mar 2, 2013 11:24am

One thing I desire is to see you, My Lord; I just want to see you in my everyday life. You have been my heart, you have been my sustenance and you have been my strength, you are my shield. You will lift me up.

I want others to see you in me at all cost. I want others, Lord, to know that I love you with an unending love and that you love me, and that I can do all things through you, because you Christ Jesus are my strength. You are the lover of my soul and I rest in you. You are Jehovah Shammah who heals all my diseases.

What a way to wake me up this morning, what a blessing to know that I have so many friends and family and churches praying for me. What a wonderful life. How can I say thank you? There is no way, except to continue to show Christ in my life at all times, and to glorify His Name.

I am going through the normal steps of Chemo treatment so yesterday was a little under the weather. Today I am better. Those who supposedly know the truth about all of this tell me my reactions are still very nominal.

Praise God for that. I will keep striving to be here at this point.

My Awesome Joe is in California this morning, headed home to Texas. He should be here Monday. He has to stop in Phoenix tomorrow and offload some of his freight. I love this man and he is my strongest supporter, and the strength I need to survive. He has already fueled and started the long drive to home. I love to just listen to him on the other end of the phone line. He comforts me, and yet when I feel bad he can tell and makes suggestions to help me.

We usually talk when I first get up in the morning, and we can be on the phone for an hour or two before we get disconnected. I am so glad we got unlimited service with the cell phones. We had it with the other, but it was costing us so much more money. We felt we could use that money to pay other bills, so had to make that switch, and the only thing I don't like is my new (so-called) smart phone. It is no match for the other one I had. But we can get me another phone in a few months I hope.

Psalm 54:4
Mar 3, 2013 11:10am

"Surely God is my help; the Lord is the one who sustains me" (Psalm 54:4 NIV), says God is my help, He IS the one who sustains me. How awesome is that. How truly wonderful to know that God sustains me, I don't have any need of fear.

I remember I used to teach the children to say, "God is my helper, I am not afraid." We used to repeat it every night at bedtime, especially if they told me they were scared of the dark or something. I am not afraid of anything.

Sometimes I get a little excited because something new is coming, but I am not afraid, just don't like surprises.

I like the surprises that bring a dozen roses to the door, or an unexpected gift to me, but I do not like surprises about my health or healthcare or selected other things. I think I am a pretty normal woman.

God has been so good to me on this journey, He has allowed me to take one step at a time, get used to that and then move on to the next step. That is how it is supposed to be. Slow and easy, so you don't have a lot of stuff to deal with all at once.

My family has been right there with me, and I love them so much for it, my friends have been invaluable in their constancy and love. You all have kept my feet firmly planted and keep reminding me that I am here for a reason. I may not understand the reason, but I know God can use it for His good, and that this will turn into a testimony, I just have to keep my head on straight. And to do that, I need God's Word dwelling inside me, growing inside me. I have to let Him shine so that He can do "Exceedingly, abundantly above all I can ask or think."

Since I had the Chemo treatments on Tuesday and Wednesday, I am more energetic than the last time, but I can still tell the difference. My face still has a yellow pallor to it; I have had some pain I am not used to, other little things. But I am still okay, and I am told that for my condition I am doing remarkably well at this stage. I like that. It means God is perfecting His work in me, not the other way around.

My sister and her son went to Peoria, Illinois for a funeral this week and they are on their way back home today. I pray God will keep them safe, and that the extended family up there will find some comfort. They really need the Lord, but I can't help that right now.

I wish I had the movie "Cars" here today. "I feel the need, the need for speed. Kachow." The party is beginning to lag a little bit.

Remember from whence your help comes and do all that you can do to show yourself approved so that when you need His help you don't have to pray all the way through before you ask. He wants a constant conversation.

You alone are my Shield
Mar 4, 2013 8:38am

2 Corinthians 7:16 says "I am glad I can have complete confidence in YOU". If we can have complete confidence in Christ then we have no problem with saying 'You alone are my Strength, my Shield.' And when we place our trust then it becomes easy to say 'To You alone may my Spirit yield.'

Complete confidence brings forth complete submission, which demonstrates that we are in complete trust (to those around us). Over the years, I have watched my parents face many situations, and my Dad and Mom always said, "If God brought us to it, then He will bring us through it." My Mom and Dad paid their tithes and did their giving where we didn't see it, they didn't believe in waving a flag. (Sometimes I wish they had taught us more about giving and tithing, but they taught us what they thought was right.) Much of their giving we wouldn't know about until we were much older. But we knew they were always doing their giving one way or another.

My parents had Complete Confidence in God to bring us through, and with that kind of training behind me, when I told my Mom about my diagnosis, she said, "Where did you get all of this faith, where did you learn to trust like this?"

It was easy, "I got it from that woman I grew up with. I called her MOM. You may not know her." She said, "You got me."

I thank my God for parents who instilled this faith in me before I was 8 years old. I have always known that so long as I let God have control, He would take care of me and never let me go.

Before we moved from Wilmer in 1969, (maybe '68) we had a music box that sat on a shelf which hadn't worked in years. We all loved it and kept it just to look at. Daddy had been praying about a situation in which he needed a definite answer, a sign to show him which way to go. He woke one night and started to the bathroom and the music box went to playing. Daddy took that as God's answer. As far as I know it never worked again, but Daddy held it in his hands that night and listened to it play, and knew God's answer to his prayer.

It isn't hard to learn faith from people who trust the Lord like that. Later, after I was grown, my mom woke one morning and felt the need to pray for me. She prayed for about an hour, and finally felt a release, and went back to sleep. She could not have known a man had broken into my apartment with the intention of raping me. My mother's prayers that night saved my life, and possibly my son's. He left with no problems. I backed him all the way out of that apartment. When your parents demonstrate that kind of faith, it's easy to learn it from them.

I love my parents, my dad went home in 1986, and Mom is married to Leon Pickens. We have known him and his family since moving to Terrell in 1969. It wasn't hard to accept him because we know he is as singularly full of faith as Mom is. When we need prayer, he stops everything to pray for us. They are still teaching us faith.

But this morning, I thought I would show you my dad. I miss him still, but I don't constantly mourn him. I am waiting my time for a great reunion in the sky. All things happen as they are supposed to so long as we exercise trust and faith in our Heavenly Father.

Blessed Assurance
Mar 5, 2013 2:26pm

Blessed assurance, Jesus is mine, Oh what a foretaste of glory divine. I'm an heir of salvation and a purchase of God, Born of His Spirit, and Washed in His Blood.

I had a rough night last night and then a short trip to town with Joe this morning. I didn't do anything but ride, but it wore me out. We came back home and I went straight to sleep. Maybe later I can wake up enough to write something.

God is always working
Mar 6, 2013 9:25am

"God is always working behind the scenes in our lives. Live in expectation, even in the midst of your trials, because He will bring forth something good from your difficulties." Debbie Kay

I AM A VICTIM OF AMAZING GRACE

One of my Facebook friends shared that she was in line to pick her child up at school this week when a man walked up to the car and said, something like, "God wants me to give you this because He cares for you." That man handed her a hundred-dollar bill and walked away.

Kind of reminds me where I was when my husband, James, died in 1997. People would come looking for me, know my name, walk into my office and ask for me, and hand me money, and one of them actually said he had driven from Pensacola, Florida to bring me a hundred-dollar bill. Others would bring me $20 or $50. God supplied my need through people who didn't even know me, and He asked them to give what they had. My need was met, and most of my family and friends didn't know what my immediate need was. He did it for about 2 months, and then, when I was ready, He stopped the flow. These people would know my first name started with an I or what it sounded like, some knew where I would be, others had to stop and ask. The point is God knew where I was and He brought my help to me when I least expected it.

When we were children, we were exposed to Scarlet Fever. There were 7 of us kids and Mom and Dad. We couldn't afford that kind of a break out. Mom said 3 or 4 of us actually ran a temperature, but Martha was the one who got it the worst. She was very young. They took us to church, First Assembly of God in Wilmer, Texas, and asked for prayer. The pastor told the congregation what was going on and we were all prayed for. Not one of those people chose to leave. Martha was burning up with fever and those people anointed her with oil and began to pray. Martha broke out in a big sweat, her fever broke, and she never had any further signs of this infection. She was healed instantly, as were the rest of us. There was never any need for Mom to take any of us to the doctor for that fever. It was gone, immediately.

I tell you this because I want you to know that I know God could have taken this cancer from me. He could have removed it instantly. He chose a path of faith for me, and it is a path I must conquer.

Yesterday was very bad, but Awesome Joe was here with me. He actually cooked for me, and that is a first in the almost 10 years we have been married. He made me scrambled eggs and smoked sausage last night. I didn't even sit up to eat, I fed myself lying down, and that's how bad I felt. Today is still shaky, but I feel better. I can't push myself too hard, that's all.

I need to work on the blanket I decided to make for Brandi, at the Chemo lab. I want to take it to her next time I go, the 27th of this month. It is perfect for her, young and alive and vibrant as she was.

Please pray for me that I may continue to do His will.

Lord I want to know You more
Mar 7, 2013 10:16am

>Lord, help me to see with Your eyes,
>Hear with Your ears,
>Speak with Your voice,
>and Heal with Your hands,
>But Mostly,
>Help me to Love with Your Heart
>AMEN

What dedication to Christ's heart. What determination we need to have before we pray that prayer. Not just empty words, but to sincerely pray that prayer. To allow God to change us to the point where we can look at others and respond to them in a way that allows them to see only Christ in our response. That last line, to love with Your heart... to love is hard for a lot of people but to love with the heart of Christ? He loved us so much He died for us. He allowed Himself to be beaten and scourged, spat upon and laughed at, and then He was nailed to a cross. After hours of agony they brought Him vinegar to drink. Imagine doing that for your friend. Yet, Jesus, because He loved us too much to call on Heaven's angels to deliver Him, Jesus stayed there. He took on all of our sins, our diseases (my lymphoma) and He stayed there. He stayed there with our hatred and our dislike and our disbelief. When He was near the end, when they could do no more to Him, then He cried, "Father, please forgive them, they know not what they do" (Luke 23:34 KJV).

Can you imagine yourself having that much love for another? Can you imagine having that much love for the people who have hurt you? Can you? This is what that prayer is asking of the Father. Let me love with your heart.

Don't let my tongue slip
Mar 8, 2013 10:27am

Dear Heavenly Father, I come to you with the boldness that the Holy Spirit gives me. I praise you for everything that I must face, and I have asked and continue to ask only that my steps on this journey bring you Glory, Honor and Praise. Father, You would clear my mind once again to hear only Your voice. I condemn every word that says I am "eat up" with cancer, and I replace it with Your Word that states if any is sick among you let them call forth the elders of the church and let them be anointed with oil and their sins shall be forgiven and they shall be healed. I choose to remember what Your Word says, "By the stripes of Jesus I am healed". I will not allow any negative thoughts or actions to get in the way of my healing and I ask that from hence forth you would seal the lips of anyone who would speak that death trap over me. I cannot hear it and continue in Your battle, this journey is You and me, Lord, and there is no room for any evil to intrude. I give you Praise, In Jesus Name, and I call it done, Amen.

It was an honest slip of the tongue, one friend describing to another who hadn't seen me in several months, that the reason I look a little peaked is because of the Chemo I am taking because I am .... With cancer. I know I have this diagnosis. I know they said it is Follicular Non-Hodgkin's Lymphoma, I know it goes from shoulders to legs; I have joked about all of that. But when she said I was ..... with cancer, everything in my brain shut down. I have had nightmares about it for 3 days. I guess technically its true, but I didn't need to be told. I don't think I needed to hear it put that way. I told Awesome Joe what a complete shock it was to hear her put it that way, and he said, "Again, no one knows how to take you, because you are so positive." In other words, I don't let on how bad it is, I prefer to speak healing into this body and allow no interference.

When you are fighting the battles of your life, you can't afford to let the negative thoughts get in there at all. You must feed your mind the Scripture and the good news. You will rarely hear me tell you how bad my day was, only that I had a rough one, because to admit it gives the evil one some sort of power over me, and I won't do that.

This is not even my battle, though my body is completely involved, this battle belongs to my Father, and to Jesus and the Holy Spirit, and if they can't fight it, I don't need anyone else's help. It's the Lord's and either way I win.

What I want, at my very next testing, is to be told the tumors are shrinking or completely gone. I want this cancer radically removed from my body. They told me it doesn't go away. You live with it. That is contrary to God's Word. And, for me, anything contrary to God's Word must be a lie straight from hell and the devil. Don't tell me what this can do to me; tell me what God can do to it.

As for me and Awesome Joe, and the rest of my family, we choose to believe that I will be healed completely. As for my friend and her slip of the tongue, well, I would be willing to bet that God already dealt with her and she is praying differently about it now. I love her, and do not want to take a chance on losing our friendship, just got to teach her to watch her thoughts.

I am so Blessed
Mar 9, 2013 9:53am

I heard a knock at the door late yesterday afternoon. When I went to answer, it was Mrs. Jane Hogg from Brookside Baptist Church. She brought me some of her homemade soup (which was delicious) and visited with me for a few minutes. That soup was so good, and sometimes I find it hard to cook for myself.

I have Corey and Sandra here, and they will cook for me, but it was quite a change to have soup. I haven't had good soup since I stopped cooking it on Saturdays the first week after I had Chemo. It was a wonderful treat.

They give me steroids to make me hungry, and I knew a loss of appetite was going to be a problem, but really, don't you have to be hungry to force feed yourself. Her soup made it easy.

There is a song which says, "God takes good care of me." and He does. He takes excellent care of me. He is my source, my strength, and my song. I am content that 'all things work together for good to those who are called according to His purpose' (Romans 8:28 KJV). Therefore (yes, Brother Jerry, I said therefore) I wait patiently for Him to do His work.

Well, its late in the day...
Mar 10, 2013 5:48pm

I am sorry., I have been dozing on and off most of the day. Just tired today, I guess. I was supposed to have company, but they didn't make it, which is probably for the best because I would have slept through their visit.

God promised He would be there with us, and that when we can see only one set of footprints He would be carrying us. I believe He is doing a lot of that lately. He carries me and lets me rest, and then when I feel like I can go He lets me stand. How wonderful is that? He loves us enough to allow that. He loves us enough to help us through the hardest times, and to stand beside us and to catch us if we begin to fall.

I've been very quiet today. Hope you all feel as blessed as I do.

Faith is...
Mar 11, 2013 9:42am

"Faith never knows where it is being led, but it loves and knows the ONE who is leading..." Oswald Chamber.

FAITH is...
FAITH
FULLY
   AND
      IMPLICITLY
      TRUSTING
         HIM......   Psalm 23

Faith is the substance of things hoped for, the evidence of things not seen.
Hebrews 11:1
Looking unto Jesus, the author and finisher of our faith, who for the joy that was set before Him endured the cross, despising the shame, and has sat down at the right hand of the throne of God. Hebrews 12:2
If you feed yourself the Scripture, the Words of God himself, then it is impossible to not have faith. Faith comes by hearing and hearing by the Word of God. Which of us can change any of our bad circumstances on our own? We cannot, we need a God who works in the miraculous

realm. We need faith to call on Him and then rest upon His answer.

That doesn't mean we can sit down and do absolutely nothing, sometimes He requires the ridiculous, sometimes the hard, and sometimes we must just verbalize our faith. For me the step of faith in this journey is to not quit, to do as the doctors say, and to take the Chemo. I didn't really want it, but I didn't hear any options from that still small voice in my head. If I want to stay here on this earth and do what He called me to do, then I must follow His leadership. All I heard was obedience. Here I am.

But, that's enough about me. Have you ever asked God why you didn't get the things you wanted? Have you ever asked Him why your need wasn't met? Read Deuteronomy 28:1-14 to Him. Read it out loud. You will be amazed.

God didn't promise to lay down the red carpet for you and make everything a total cake walk. What He promised was that if you would walk in obedience to His commands, these blessings will come upon you and overtake you (watch the football player tackle the runner with the ball heading toward the end zone). He named blessing upon blessing. Sometimes you have to remind Him that you know your promises and you always have to let the enemy know that you know your promises.

Years ago, when my son and his family were not serving the Lord, I put a picture of them in a frame, and matted it and underneath the picture I wrote, "Even the fruit of my body shall be blessed" (Deuteronomy 28:11 KJV). Every time I walked by that picture I called my son in and declared to God Almighty that he was blessed because of my obedience. That's what the Bible says. It didn't matter what he was doing, that promise is contingent on my actions.

A few years later, he had to have an emergency appendectomy and was off work for about 3 months. No Pay. My daughter-in-law called me one day and told me they had no food for the 4 children and themselves and she didn't know what they were going to do. I hung up the phone and started praying. I reminded God of His promise to bless them, and I told Him if I was doing something wrong He had permission to change me, otherwise He needed to bless my children. I was pushy because I needed to get an immediate answer.

She called me back a few hours later and told me that the elderly lady across the street had brought them 4 bags of frozen meat. She was a vegetarian, she said, and her children were trying to force her to eat meat. They brought it to her and she wanted to make sure someone would eat it. That is God's blessing, His provision.

I always ask God to look at me, to search me, and if I am wrong to change me, but if not to honor His promise. Sometimes I do have to change my actions or words, because I give Him permission to convict me if I need changing. That's faith. Walk in it, talk it, it works.

He has never failed me yet, He will not fail me ever, and all I ever need to do is call His name. Be blessed today.

Here I am, Lord, Use me
Mar 12, 2013 9:34am

The greater perfection a soul aspires after, the more dependent it is upon divine grace.
What a beautiful thought. We are totally dependent upon divine grace to be perfect, and yet it is something we can never attain on this earth.

Well, yesterday was probably the busiest day I have had in over 2 months. God knows when we can stand not one more minute of our own company for a while. First, 2 ladies from The Barn Fellowship came by and brought me a plant and visited with me for a while. Then I had 2 separate families come by for food, each taking the time to check on me in their time of need. Then, my parents came and brought Breezy, my niece to visit. After they left, my friend from Edgewood, Sue Harber, came by for a visit and to drop off some food for the ministry. Breezy cooked for me. My parents returned, hoping to catch a short visit with my last visitors of the day. My son and his entire family came by. They got here at 7:45 and stayed until about 9:30. Corey and Sandra were here also. That's a lot of people for little ole me, but I was about to go cabin crazy and I guess God knew that. I hadn't seen my son's family in a few months because every time we planned a visit from them someone would get sick.

It was such a pleasure to see all of them, and then, after they all left, I just collapsed into the bed. Breezy stayed up for a while, and when Awesome Joe arrived home at 2:45 this morning, we all got up and had a late-night snack and then peach pie and ice cream. Back to bed.

I feel blessed this morning, just because my Father knows my needs so well. I could easily start pulling my hair out when the house gets too quiet. Thankfully, they were all very careful to not tire me and to allow me to sit and rest, and I had time between visits to rest.

Joe and I are going to spend today together and Breezy asked if she could go with us. I am riding in the vehicle today. Tomorrow is my 2 weeks after chemo date, so I feel pretty safe by now.

If I pray the prayer of Jabez, then I will be asking the Lord to lead me to any chance to witness today. I think that is a good place to start. I am so excited at what God is doing in my body. Everybody be blessed and have a great day. I love you all.

He is Awesome
Mar 13, 2013 9:42am

As I left you yesterday, I said as in the prayer of Jabez, "Just give me one person to witness to." He answered quickly. At our first stop, Denny's, we ran into an old friend. She had not heard that I had this cancer. When she saw the PICC line in my arm, she started to cry and to tell me how sorry she was. I was able, immediately, to witness to her and her friend how my faith works and that we are very humbled to be on this journey. See, I know how much my Father must trust me, to give me this test.

By the time we left, we were all talking about the funny things in this, and we were laughing, and she was much encouraged. God answered me quickly and gave me my ONE person to witness to. He is always faithful to answer our prayers, especially when our prayers are to honor HIM.

What good would it do me to go on this journey if I didn't learn my lessons and finish the journey? A pastor once told me you have to conquer it, or it keeps coming back until you are strong enough to get all the way through. Well I am trying to listen, to learn and to be the person He wants me to be in all of this. If you hear anything to the contrary, please forgive me. Sometimes my human side forgets for a moment.

Pastor Jerry Truett told me a few weeks ago that my Scripture at this time is (Ephesians 3:20-21 NKJV). "Now unto Him who is able to do Exceedingly, Abundantly above all that we ask. According to the power that works in us, to Him be glory in the church by Christ Jesus to all generations forever and ever, amen."

When amplified, I believe it means that God can do over and above anything we even have the ability to think to ask for. Every time you read the Word of God, your thoughts become more and more like His thoughts. Then your desires begin to line up with His Word and His plans for you. You reach a point where, before you even think it, or realize you might need it, God has already provided. He does exceedingly, ABUNDANTLY over and above everything we can ask or think. When I asked for my healing, He had more than that in mind. Before the doctor told me I was sick, He had already made provision for me.

The point is, we must read the Word, strive to be more like Him and in tune with Him. Then when these things arise we are supposed to conform to His will for us, not waddle in our own filth and pity.

I didn't just get born with this faith, I had to really work hard, and I've been tested and tried. And I have failed. Sometimes we learn by trial and error. When you fail, understanding that you are human, you must forgive yourself and get up and go forward. The test will come again. You just have to keep on learning and keep pressing forward. You will come back around to the test again and you will be stronger and more ready to pass it.

Sometimes the test is your first response; we are supposed to be instant with our answer and always able to give an answer for the confidence within us. My answer is easy, I believe that God created the earth and that He created man (and woman) in His own image. I believe that Adam and Eve fell and were cursed with death, which is for all humankind, and were sent out of the Garden of Eden. I believe that God sent His only Son, Jesus to be born of a virgin, to grow and to be crucified for the remission of our sins. I believe that by His stripes I am healed, as is anyone else who believes, and that because I believe, because my faith stays strong, I can ask, and He will answer. And I believe that His answer may not always be the one I want to hear, but it will always be the one that is absolutely HIS BEST FOR ME.

Mrs. Pat, thank you for your prayers. That means so much to me, I love you.

God's plans
Mar 14, 2013 10:40am

"God's thoughts are the thoughts to think, God's Words are the Words to speak, and God's ways are the ways to act." Kenneth Copeland.

Praise the Almighty God. It has been a very busy week for this homebound patient. I have had visitors, and friends from everywhere. Even the children who have come have needed to understand (and they've done very good with it) that I allow no negative thoughts or words AT ALL in this house, especially about my disease. If it isn't written in the Book, don't say it in the house. That doesn't mean I am blind. It just means that I am not allowing the negative to exist here. I am thinking God's thoughts and saying God's Words, and I try very hard to act as God would act in this situation.

That isn't always easy, but I can tell you that I am not suffering like a lot of other people I know. It's probably a very good thing, because I can't take a lot of pain medicines, mostly non-addictive, non-narcotic. Therefore, I am very thankful that when I do need something the ones that work on my Fibromyalgia also help with the other. The doctor was very surprised when I told him I was not in need of anything else at this time. It could be, of course, I've lived with this pain for so long that I don't recognize the difference, but either way I am so glad I have not needed anything really strong. I don't know what they would be able to give me.

I have taken the nausea medicines a few times, but always more as a preventative than because I can't stop. Basically, if I begin to feel nauseated, I will take one, before it goes any further.

I would say my reactions are still very nominal and for that I give praise, honor and glory to my Father, God, and to Jesus the KING of KINGS. I thank Him because I am healed in Jesus Name and this is a minor inconvenience on the way to perfect health.

I trust you will all have a great day, and PLEASE be sure to sign my guest book. I can't believe I already have 525 visits, but there are few signatures. Be blessed. I love you all.

FRIDAY!!!!!!!
Mar 15, 2013 5:54pm

I have to say I went to doctor this morning, and I'm impressed with God's work in me. It's pretty awesome. This was my regular doctor. He had asked me to come back after a few treatments, so he could check me for problems. He told me I am doing absolutely great and that he was impressed with my position at this point in my treatment. We discussed my faith, and I told him it wasn't a question of how long I have to live, but rather -- how long I have to take the treatments before I can get back to my life. I told him God is the only one who has my days numbered and He is doing really great with me, and nobody else can control it. I also told the doctor, I believe in healing, but that we must temper our faith with wisdom to get the results God wants us to have.

All I can say is, in the words of a song, "God takes good care of me."

I will be fine in a day or two,
Mar 17, 2013 4:08pm

I had granddaughter and two nieces and another girl to spend Friday night. That's enough for a healthy person, much less one trying to recover from chemo. They wore me plum, completely out. I did think I would have some help from others, but that didn't quite work out, so I was on my own. One or two of them would probably have been fine, and I could have controlled the situation, but the truth is the fourth little girl I don't know. She didn't go to sleep; she doesn't necessarily do as told. All in all, it was too much for me.

They had fun, because they had a fingernail party in the afternoon, and then went skating, but to spend the night.... well that was a disaster. 2:30 is too late to be fighting girls to get them to sleep. My granddaughter was asleep by 11:30. The other 3... Whew. And I told them to go to bed. They just didn't understand that I meant business.

The fourth girl left about 10:30 Saturday morning; my 2 nieces left around 2 and took my granddaughter with them. By then I was shaking with tiredness and ready for relief. I took 4 pain pill and 3 muscle relaxers on Saturday and got up this morning and had to take more medicines. Hopefully it won't take me too very long to recover my strength. I told that fourth girl that she can't return to my house until she learns to behave herself.

I hated missing church this morning, but I didn't even wake up until after 10, and since church was already started that's a little bit late.

The good news is I got to spend quality time with my granddaughter and that time is precious to me. She is about to be a teenager and then you get less and less time as you go along, until eventually you are begging for time. I love that child so much. She's coming back on Friday and is planning to stay and go to church with me on Sunday. Just me and her, that's what I want.

I can only take so much stress and then I tire out and start yelling and going crazy on them. Now, instead of a single day to recover, it may take me 3 or 4.

Anyway, God is good, and I got to spend time with them. That's important to me. My family means so much to me, and spending time together is so very important. We live so far apart, that when we get a chance we just have to do it. He always gives me rest when I need it.

God is my strength and my shield. I simply have to trust Him to know what is best for me, and I can't do that with the girls again for a while. I think I just forgot that I wasn't top of my game for a bit. I remember now.

My nephew, Clevern, turned 30 this weekend and my brother and sister-in-law are in town from Kentucky.

I can't wait to see them. They had a dinner for him last night, but I didn't make it. They have promised to come by and see me, and so I think probably tomorrow.

Keep your eyes on Jesus, Keep the road before you straight, and never forget where you are going. God is watching you at all times, and He will carry you. I love you and will write more tomorrow.

Oh, What a Beautiful Morning
Mar 18, 2013 9:50am

The temperature outside is 68 Fahrenheit. I can handle that when I wake up. In fact, I absolutely love it, no heat and no air conditioning. Just dwell in what God gives us and no need to change a thing. My verse for today was "May the God of Hope fill you with all joy and peace as you trust in Him, so that you may overflow with hope by the power of the Holy Spirit" (Romans 15:13 NIV).

Hallelujah, I do serve a God of Hope, and I feel much better today. And I have promised my wonderful husband that I won't do that again without having at least one other adult with me, so that when I get tired I can skip out of the mess.

T D Jakes posted on Facebook this morning, "Spend more time preparing for where you will end up. It's just a process that you are going through to get you to the next level." I had to put the soup ministry on hold, but not the food ministry, for a few months while I walk this journey, but I am preparing myself to come back stronger and with an even larger presence in this area. These people need to know that God has not forgotten them and that He will take care of them, and that He has the power to change their situations.

The God that I serve will not let me down. He knows where my heart is; and He knows what we need to do for His people here.

I love you all. My brother is on his way to see me and I have to get dressed for them.

Wonderful Week. ...
Mar 20, 2013 4:55pm

With Cleve and Joann here from Kentucky, my house has been abuzz all week. Joe was here Tuesday, and I slept in the afternoon. But my family was here on Monday, 9 of us, we all ate at Denny's. Then Joe came in late evening, and was here all-day Tuesday, Cleve and Jo came back on Tuesday and she cleaned my kitchen and vacuumed the living room, then today Cleve and Alfred (my brother from Longview) were here along with my parents. Today we ate Pizza out on the porch.

I have to send a big thank you to Corey and Sandra because without them I would be lost here. He won't even let anyone else refill my glass with water. She cleaned for us; he brought chairs out and then brought them back inside. They take such good care of me.

This weather has been so beautiful, and we were able to enjoy the outdoors as well as the inside. With the floors cleaned, I felt more comfortable and was able to relax while they were all here. I have so enjoyed seeing my brothers and Joann. It is so hard for all of us to get together. But God is good to me, and He orchestrated a week of fun and time, and even the weather was good. I am so very blessed.

Blessings... exceedingly, abundantly
Mar 21, 2013 9:57am

I love my family so much, and what a wonderful blessing for it all to work out while I was in my 2 weeks break here from being basically confined to the house. This week I have seen my brothers, my sisters-in-law, my parents, we have talked and hugged and loved each other. It has been a good time together.

As my youngest brother was leaving yesterday, and he returns to Kentucky tomorrow, he said if he didn't already know I was sick, he couldn't tell by looking. That was the sweetest thing anyone could say to me right now. Sometimes I look in the mirror and see a different me. But he said I look perfectly normal. I love that.

I go back to Chemo next week, 27th and 28th, after that I won't look normal for about 10 days. But right now, in the mirror, I look normal.

Destiny is coming for the weekend, and I can't wait to see her. She is growing up so fast. She will be 13 in June, and my times get further and further apart as she grows up.

I remember when she was a child and she would come to me and crawl up on me, and Dewayne and Libby would try to put her down for sleep, she would come straight back to me. They said they didn't want her to learn to sleep with anyone, and I had to tell them I'm not anyone, I'm grandma. I am not here all the time. Leave her alone and we will sleep together. It was always so relaxing just to have her close to me. Now she's all ready for the world, she thinks, and I have to fight tooth and nail to get a few days with her. I treasure these days. She goes through my jewelry, she wears my hats, and she can now wear my shoes. Luckily my clothing is still way too big for her, but she has made a couple of my sweaters look good over her clothes. I love her so much. She told me last week she is trying out for cheerleader, which will make it even harder for her to see me.

God has been good to me, and when I say I hear Him coming, I am looking for His return to take us home to live with Him forever, but I enjoy just relaxing in His presence. I can turn on the soft praise music and rest in it and know that He is constantly working on me to make me perfect, in body and Spirit.

Because of Who You Are
Mar 22, 2013 11:03am

>Lord, Because of Who You Are I give you glory,
>Because of Who You are I give you praise,
>Because of Who You are I will worship and adore,
>Lord, I Worship You Because of Who You Are....

Jehovah Jireh, my provider, Jehovah Nissi, Lord you reign in Victory, Jehovah Shalom you are my peace, Jehovah Raphah, my healer.

One of my dear friends came by last night (I had a stressful day with personal matters) and we had prayer for about 30 minutes. We got my brother on the phone and he prayed with us some. That is the best stress relief I have ever found.

I start Chemo again on Wednesday the 27th, and Thursday the 28th. I know that sometime soon they will schedule me for test to see how this is working. I trust in my

Fathers Word and believe for my healing. Can't wait to get good results, but not sure at what point they re-do the tests.

What a Way to Praise God
Mar 23, 2013 8:26am

I woke early with a song on my mind, one that my friend, Barbara, in Memphis used to sing. She would say, "I just can't give up now, I've come too far from where I started from. Nobody told me the road would be easy, but I don't believe He's brought me this far to leave me." Mary-Mary didn't exist yet. This is an old Spiritual. They made it well known, but Barbara taught it to me before them. I love that song. He brought me way too far for me to ever think about turning back.

Now, I am listening to this... "Take my mind, conform it, take my will transform it to Yours, To Yours, O Lord." I believe we must transform our minds and our hearts to be in agreement with His thoughts and His plans for us. The only way to do that is to spend time with Him daily, morning, noon, and night. He wants it all. He doesn't want a show of time this morning, and then do what we want all day. He wants our time. He wants us to realize that every word we speak goes to Him. No matter who we are speaking to, every word we speak goes up to Him. We can't love Him, and curse those He has made. You can't make a show of spending time with Him, unless He is actually transforming you into what He wants you to be. He says blessing for curses, love for hurts, and forgiveness.

Unfortunately, we are human, and we get off track, but it is much easier to be Christ like when we are living, eating and breathing the Word of God. When He truly dwells in us, then His Words come alive in us. Then we are truly TRANSFORMED into what He wants us to be, an image of Him.

Now, let us go forth and praise Him with a New Song, plant your feet on the Rock and don't be shaken. Let every Word you speak come from Him.

Destiny didn't make it this weekend; she got a chance to go to Six Flags. I can't compete with that. Unfortunately, the storms may destroy their day. I didn't pray for that, I really didn't. I wanted to see her, but I would never wish her to be unhappy.

It just turned totally dark here; I think I should get off line for a while.

I'm ready
Mar 24, 2013 7:48pm

Pastor Jerry Truett asked us 2 questions this morning:

1 Do you have a personal relationship with Jesus Christ?

And then after his sermon:

2. Do you love Jesus for Who He is or for what He can do for you?

I find the answers to these questions easy, because I have worked on them all of my life, but I know others may not be at that point. I love the Lord for Who He is and for all that He HAS done for me. From the beginning of time, to Jesus death on the Cross, to now, I love Jesus because He first loved me. I love Him because without Him I can't even walk.

I do not expect Him to do anything for me. He is not a God who performs on demand. He is a God who keeps His promises, who always loves me no matter what I do. He is a God who refuses to let me fall, and who always extends His hands when I can't do anything on my own.

I am very comfortable with praising Him no matter what goes wrong or right with me here. In fact, no matter what happens, so long as I try my best to be obedient to Him and follow His plan for me, then nothing that happens to me will ever be wrong. His plan for me is right, no matter where it takes me or how hard the journey is.

Today I have felt very tired. Woke up pale this morning, and figured I better put some color on my face before I went out into the world. My arm is very sore today for some reason, and I can feel a pull there at the point of insertion of the PICC line. I have to be able to go through Chemo again on Wednesday and Thursday, so I just need to listen to Him and make sure I get plenty of rest before then.

Please examine your heart and make sure you are in line with those two questions. I can't think of anything that will matter more when we get to the end of the line, and when I cross that river I want it to be right.

I wish you would sign my guestbook, I love to know who and how many are here. It really encourages me, even if all you say is HI.

Isaiah 53
Mar 25, 2013 12:15pm

He (Jesus) was wounded for our transgressions, He was bruised for our iniquity, the chastisement of our sin was upon Him, and by His stripes we are healed (Isaiah 53:5 NKJV).

I memorized that verse as a child in Missionettes, the Assembly of God's girls' group at the time, and it has always been important to me. Right now, at this time in my life, I find it means so much more. I have considered all that went on in the week leading up to Jesus' crucifixion. He rode into Jerusalem on a donkey, with the people gathering in His path to line it with praise, adoration, and palm branches. They were so excited that the Master had come to them.

Unfortunately, as Pastor Jerry Truett pointed out yesterday and I have known for years, He refused to perform on demand. He was not a paid performer, such as our musicians and idols of today; He was Jesus, The Son of God, The Son of Mary and Joseph, man and God in one. He could not, would not turn the work of God into a spectacle for the gathered multitudes. They turned on Him.

This is what we do so often. We serve Him, because of what He is supposed to do for us according to the teachings of the modern world. Unfortunately for us, He is not a God who is moved by popular demand, He can't be bought. He has a plan and He works it so long as we allow Him to do so.

I could have demanded an instant healing to my body, but I didn't. I only want Glory to Him, and to praise and communicate with Him. I could listen to the people who said I don't have to go through this, but that might not be God's plan for my life. I could be foolish and refuse to take the doctor's instructions to heart. But I firmly believe God gave us a brain so that we could think and use HIS wisdom in these matters.

I could have even turned on HIM and looked at the world and said what the world said to me, 'You are dying'. But I refuse to do that, and I refuse to give up.

I plan to let God work His plan for my life, and I pray that my life will bring Him glory. I pray that people will see Him in me, and not me. I want to reflect Him to the world.

By His Stripes
Mar 26, 2013 8:55am

The Bible says that BY HIS STRIPES WE WERE HEALED. It does not say we can be healed, or we will be healed. It says we were healed. That is past tense.

I met a lady last night who told me several times that God was going to heal her. Her story made mine look very simple. But there is a huge difference in believing that we will be healed, and we were already healed. Sometimes we have to walk a journey. Sometimes we have to be tested. But the answer is always the same. I was healed by the stripes on Jesus back, as they were getting Him ready for crucifixion.

I don't need to know what is going to happen in the future. I don't need to hear how bad the prognosis is. What I need is to know over and over again that Jesus ALREADY did it. He did it. He knew exactly what they would diagnose as Follicular Non-Hodgkin's Lymphoma, and He took it to the grave with Him. He killed it there. He took it to Hell and took the diagnosis and the disease with Him and left it there when He arose triumphantly over death, Hell, and the grave.

I don't have to live with this. I told the other lady that. I may have to go through this journey, I may have to walk the walk and talk the talk, but I do NOT have to cave in to this diagnosis. Praise God.

I told this to the lady who was sitting behind me. I told her to start saying it right. And I told her I stand with her in believing that she is healed…

At this point I began to get frustrated…

Now WHAT?
Mar 27, 2013 4:35pm

I did everything I could to be right, but Joe and Marie and even the kids had noticed that I was dragging. I just thought I was trying to do too much, but that wasn't the case. Actually, the chemo caused my immunity to go way down, and now I have to give the shot a week to work before I can go back next week and do Chemo.

It was disappointing for the doctor to tell me that, especially since I actually had felt better the past two weeks (except for being so tired). I put on a little makeup Sunday because my face looked very pale. But then that happens with Chemo. So, I wasn't worried.

They told me when I started this journey that my CNC had to stay above 1500 or I would be taking shots. The first reading was 2700, then 3300, then 2400. I have eaten all the right things. I have avoided crowds. Up until the granddaughter came, I didn't even let myself get tired. Today's reading was 800, which is nowhere near 1500. He said that's why I feel tired. DUH. I had that one figured out really fast.

On the way home, I told my friend I am not a patient person and I want to stand and stomp my feet and say, "I want my healing and I want it NOW" because my patience with this stuff is gone. But I can't do that because I gave this to my Father and told Him I will do whatever He asks of me, so long as He gets the glory. Well I was reminded of that very quickly, and heard this

"I can't heal you RIGHT NOW, because you said I could have the GLORY and it's not time yet." Okay, then. My patience will be stronger by next week.

Feeling tired and wanting to sleep today thus will make this a short message. I love you all.

CHAPTER NINE

Cancer brings forth every negative thought you ever had in your life. It becomes a demon, and if you let it, cancer will steal every small bit of your peace, and as a raging lion, it takes over your life. I did not want this to happen. I was so certain everything was good that I got frustrated and wanted to complain. I really am human, after all. Very few of my family and friends actually saw this come out in me. Marie saw it because she was there. Joe saw it and heard it, but he lives with me.

Those who saw me every now and then did not see this, and that's why, every now and then, when I would actually say anything at all, my wonderful husband and Marie would kick me back into gear. Marie Sims took such good care of me that Joe was not worried when he was on the road and could not be here. I am so very thankful to the two of them, and for the two of them. They stood beside me and, when I couldn't do it on my own, they worked around me.

Most people who know me do not know what we went through. Our very way of life was threatened. Months later, someone else had cancer, and the community pulled together to raise money for the family. I didn't want to complain; I didn't want to stop helping people, but that really hurt me. My friends were all out there doing everything they could to help raise money for her, and no one did that for me. No one even offered. I finally told Joe what I was feeling, and he just looked at me. "There you go again. You smile, you laugh, you praise the Lord, and then you look at me and wonder why no one understood how very difficult things can actually be for you. You trusted God to get you through it, now you want to know why no one offered any financial help. We made it."

I felt small when he said that. Sometimes I think I should be more painfully honest with people, but then I have to remind myself very quickly that only God can supply the need. He's the only one that I will ever need to know the complete truth. We have tithed, and we have given, and now God is taking care of us, just like His Word says He will. You see (Luke 6:38 NKJV); "Give and it shall be given unto you, good measure, pressed down and shaken together, for with what measure you mete out it shall be measured unto you." He keeps His promises. He honors every contract.

This book is so much of my heart and soul that I can't seem to stop. I only pray that, when it is finally finished, and I can rest, I want it to touch lives, and change the way people think. I am so serious about this. I want every single person to know that your life is beaten out by the words that come out of your mouth. Not the thoughts, but by the spoken word. It is so easy to be deceived, but God will perform His Word in your life if you speak it out. The tongue is a very powerful weapon, and it can also hold life and death. You do not have need to speak every thought. Speak the Word over your situation. The Word of God will perform that which it is sent for. Speak God's truth over your life, not the death sentence or horrible life that the doctors, bankers, newsmen, or teachers tell you to expect.

When we first met, I was an assistant manager at a fast food restaurant. Joe was driving his truck and he had a team driving a second truck. As soon as he asked me to marry him, I turned in my resignation so that I would be free to drive with him. I love driving and it loves me. When we married, it was just the two of us out there on the road.

Joe told me he would take care of me, and he did. I wanted for nothing while we were out there.

My husband, James, had died in 1997 and I was very secure in who I was, and what God could and would do for me. I actually told God in 1997 that I did not need a man at all. Jesus is all any of us ever need. It is nice to have a companion, and to be held, but we don't necessarily need it. We need Jesus. I promised Him that He could be my companion, my best friend, my provider and my source. I spent a lot of time just getting to know Jesus more intimately. It was just me and Him and the friends around me.

When Joe asked me to marry him, I did not hesitate. I wanted that intimacy with him. Our problem was that some other people did not think he needed to be with me. His friends were copacetic with our marriage, but his family was different. Many thought I was marrying him for his money. That was not true, and as a matter of fact I tried to find the money they were fighting him over. There was none. He had trucks, not money.

For six months I waited for him to put my name on the checkbook, or to do anything else that would tell them he trusted me. I became a complaining, raging, idiot of a nagging woman. Every time we talked it was about him 'taking care' of me. I just couldn't believe or accept the fact that everything we had was his, not mine.

(Technically, half of everything he earned was mine, by law, but he would not put my name on it.)

One morning about six months after we married, the Lord woke me up. He wanted to know what I was doing. I played dumb, even though I knew immediately what He was referring to. This was so strong that I ended up outside my house at three in the morning walking and talking to Him. He reminded me that I told Him He was my provider. I said that was true, but when a woman gets married the man becomes her provider. He asked me where I came up with that. He taught me a hard lesson that day. In fact, I was still awake around six o'clock in the morning. I called Joe to apologize to him. He was asleep but answered the phone quickly. I had been at home sick for a few weeks, actually had gall bladder surgery.

I apologized to him for all the things I had said and done. I told him he could not be my provider and that I had already given that position to God himself. He was okay with that. Then I said, "Just please promise me that whatever God asks you to do for me you will do."

Instantly, there was peace. I felt washed and clean. I felt like hundreds of pounds had fallen off of my shoulders. We were at peace and I was finally free to just love my husband. I can't tell you I am perfect. I am not. I am human, and I am sometimes very selfish. But, I will tell you that I try to listen as the Holy Spirit leads and I try to be obedient. This flesh will get in the way, but when He speaks to me I try to listen and to be corrected without a lot of complaining because, after all, I told Him He could do that.

Thursday, before Good Friday.
Mar 28, 2013 8:50am

Have you ever wondered why they call it GOOD Friday? When this is the day our Savior was crucified, when this is the day of his death? I haven't been able, in my lifetime to come up with a good answer to this. Today is the day we see Pilate wash his hands and say, "His blood be upon you, I want no part of it," They beat him with the cat of nine tails and put 39 stripes on His back, one for every disease that will ever come against mankind, they stripped him of His clothing and cast lots for His robe. Today, they did all of that. Tomorrow, Good Friday, is the day they would march Him up Calvary's Hill, and nail Him to a cross. Tomorrow is the day they put those huge nails in his hands and feet and gave Him vinegar to drink. Tomorrow, GOOD FRIDAY is the day that Jesus would die for us. Why do we call it GOOD FRIDAY?

I have no doubt the Jews called it Good Friday, because they didn't believe He was the King of the Jews, the Promised Redemption. I am wondering today why we, as Christians, can call it Good Friday. I can only come up with one answer, and it makes me very sad indeed. Is this Good Friday because it's the day He died for us? And if it's Good Friday because this is the day Jesus died for us, then why do so many in the world continue on with their ordinary lives, and celebrate in such Ungodly ways? People will get drunk; they will go to the lake and have parties. They will Barbeque, and they will do all they can to party. Why don't we cover our heads with shame and ask God's forgiveness for what we did to His Only Begotten Son? How can we look in the mirror and say, 'it's Good Friday, I can celebrate with everyone else'?

Oh sure, I believe we should be happy that He came, but do we really need to celebrate the reason for today? I think not. I think this should be a day of inner search. Looking inward to see if we have done all we can to repay Him. We can never repay Him, but we can at least serve Him and let Him know how much we appreciate HIS sacrifice.

Right now, when I need this healing so much, I wonder if there is more I can do to serve Him. I wonder if I have done all I can to show Jesus to those around me. I want others to see Him in every breath that I take. I want to show Him at all times, not me but Christ in me.

I feel much better today but am not planning to leave the house. With my immunity this low, I dare not take chances. I do love you all and would cherish visitors.

Help is on the Way
Mar 29, 2013 10:51am

So, it's Friday. Today we celebrate (or honor) Our Saviors death on Calvary. The skies grew dark, the veil was torn, the earth shook, and when all was over, there He was. Jesus, the redemption of the World, was hanging on the cross, DEAD. It was coming time for Passover and in order to obey the law of the Jews, they put Him in the tomb without dressing his body. They would return on Sunday to do that. Sunday... is on its way.

Jesus was dead for 3 days, according to Bible, He was laid in the tomb on Friday, and they covered the entrance of the tomb with a large rock that it would take several men to move. They placed guards outside the tomb to make sure no one would come in and steal the body, because He said He would RISE AGAIN.

For the time that He was there, I am almost certain He rested first, because He had been put through a lot. His hands and feet were pierced by nails; His side was pierced with the sword to make sure He was dead. Before they hung Jesus on the cross they beat Him with the Cat of Nine tails, a torturous, horrible instrument that ripped His skin to shreds. His head must have ached from the crown of thorns they put on His head. He was bruised and bloody, but not one bone was broken. That's what the Bible says.

So, Hell started a celebration. We have killed Him, Jesus the King of the Jews, and now we can rule and reign. Death, disease, addictions, ... Oh, yes, they had plans for us. And they had won, they thought. But Satan knew the truth. He was there when the Book was written. Satan knew that death and the grave could not hold our King, our Savior, and our Redemption. The price was paid in full. In the midst of their celebration, while all the demons of hell were dancing in joy, that's when they heard His voice roar like a caged lion. He began to come through the gates. Satan foolishly thought he could stop Him, "Shut and lock the gates," he cried, "don't let Him through." Satan was too late. Jesus walked triumphantly through that crowd and looked Satan in the eye.

"I'LL TAKE MY KEYS NOW!" and I believe He ripped them from Satan's limp hand. Instantly, it was Sunday morning. Instantly, it was a day of freedom and celebration for Christians everywhere. Never again would we need to be oppressed by Satan and his demons. WE ARE NOW FREE!

The KING OF GLORY, the ONE who conquered death and the grave, bought it with HIS life.

HALLELUJAH! He left every disease mankind would ever know in that grave. Every disease, every addiction, every sin, is gone. Well, friends, Sunday is on the way.

I had a really bad day of pain yesterday, not sure if I reacted to the shot they gave me or if I just felt bad. I will talk to doctor about it next week. But what I do know is that Jesus already took care of me. I gave this to HIM and I am not going to take it back. He already has it, and He will get the GLORY when my healing is made manifest.

SUNDAY IS ON THE WAY

Before you ask....
Mar 30, 2013 10:08am

My mom called early this morning to ask me how I feel. She beat Awesome Joe today, which is extremely rare, because my mom usually sleeps very late. But today she was up at the crack of dawn. It is Easter weekend, and everyone seems to be doing more than usual.

I had walked through the house and let April out for her morning catch up, fed the cat and uncovered the bird, not quite open eyed yet. The time was 9:05. I am usually up between 6:30 and 7:00 but have gone back to the first week after the first chemo. SLEEP ALL THE TIME. Yesterday, I slept so hard all day that I was certain I would not sleep last night, but I was wrong. I never moved until after 8 am this morning. The cat came and got on my feet. I suppose Corey had let him in.

I can't tell you how I feel. There is none of the horrible pain I experienced on Thursday, but sleep is fully entrapped inside my body. The first week after the first chemo treatment I slept 18 to 20 hours a day, and with the shot he gave me on Wednesday I am back to doing that. I sure am glad there is someone else here to cook, because I have no desire to do it. (I was in so much pain Thursday evening that I threatened to go to emergency, but finally got it eased down). I think the shot he gave me set off a chain reaction, but since then my body is sleeping. If that's what it takes to rebuild my blood, then so be it.

I do know that God is working a plan, and that His plan is perfect, so I will walk through the flame and I know He will not give me more than I can bear.

Because of the fatigue and the sleepiness, I will make today short. Happy Easter Weekend everybody, and remember Christ is why we are here... not the Easter bunny.

I love you.

Happy Easter
Mar 31, 2013 1:09pm

I feel much stronger today but can tell that I still have a way to go before I can run around again.

Happy Easter, remember today that Jesus died for our redemption and He rose again to seal that redemption in Heaven. He arose, that we could be free from sin, sickness, and death. Praise Him.

April Fool's Day
Apr 1, 2013 10:56am

I can't go through today without remembering how horrible my siblings and I were to MOM one year on April fool's Day. She was in bed sick (bad flu or something) when we left for school. As we walked, we planned and set in motion our actions. On the way home, we finalized all the plans. One of us ran through the house calling for mom to get out, the house is on fire. The rest of us ran to the back porch and began screaming and throwing things at the porch (like we were using our jackets or books to try to put it out). We didn't truly appreciate our Mom enough back then. She ran to the back of the house and met us at the door. She was scared silly and I think she almost fainted, but we were too busy laughing and saying, "April Fools".

··•·———•———·•··

Chemo
Apr 3, 2013 6:17am

I am on my way to Chemo today. Have to be in Tyler at 8:30 to get started. Awesome Joe was home yesterday, and he ran around most of the day, didn't stop until after 4, and then we had to have supper and relax at home. I so enjoy my time with him, but I am worn out this morning. When they give me that first dose of Benadryl, to prevent allergic reaction, I am down for the count. I will be in bed early tonight.

He got his call at 3:30 this morning and walked out the door here at 5 am. I know he will be back next week, but I miss him already. God is good to give us a little time together. He actually helped me pick out fingernail polish yesterday.

May God carefully bless each of you to what you are ready for.

Home and off to rest
Apr 3, 2013 6:18pm

Chemo went well. I slept a lot because they start with 25 mg of Benadryl straight into the infusion line. God has been good today, and we have been able to witness healing and pray with 4 different people about their cancer situation. Not a shy day for Chemo Lab.

Dr. says my CNC # is back to 1400. They want a minimum of 1500, but I got the Chemo anyway, and I go back in on Friday (after another treatment tomorrow) and they will give me another shot. That one is a good one for about 2 weeks. I am anxious to see how he wrote this one up. I may have to go back in 2 weeks for more labs. He also told me that the shot they are giving me can cause extreme pain in the bones because it tells the bone marrow to create white blood cells. I certainly do wish he had told me that last week. Now all I can do is wait.

If you haven't shared Jesus with someone today is it because you missed your chance, or do you still have time to do it?

Love to all.

God is good...
Apr 4, 2013 2:33pm

I am so thrilled that God goes into that chemo lab with me and takes good care of me. I have met a few people who are having bad reactions to the chemo treatment and have to be given shots for the nausea and stuff. I am so thankful I don't have that problem. My friend and I have talked to two people this week that have been told to put their affairs in order because they have less than 6 months to live. Both of them have told us that God is in charge and they yield to His will, but they aren't leaving here without HIM, so the doctors will have to be patient with them. AMEN

I heard one of the nurses say the other day that you can't work in that department long if you don't believe in God. You just don't last, because the miracles they see couldn't be anything else.

Pastor Jerry Truett told me to memorize Ephesians 3:20 NKJV, a few weeks ago. He told me to memorize, apply it, and repeat it over and over. "Unto Him who is able to do exceedingly abundantly above all we ask or think, according to the power that works within us."

According to my faith, so be it, I am healed by the stripes and wounds that Jesus took to Calvary. AMEN

One more Trip
Apr 5, 2013 9:47am

I have to go to Tyler again today for a short visit to get a shot to rebuild my blood count. I am so thankful that God goes with me on these trips because they wear me out. After today, I am not scheduled to return until May 1, so I get to rest up and rebuild my strength.

My Awesome Joe is a brick in a solid wall; he holds my hand (by phone) and reminds me to keep my head up. He doesn't get down and discouraged when he is with me, and he helps me to stay strong. I love him.

My friend who is here with me to help me this week, does as much for me as I will let her, but I try to do all I can. I am hard-headed; my grandson helps me when she is not here. All my other friends and family have helped me so much. How can I begin to thank you all?

No words would ever be enough. Nothing I could ever say would be enough.

I am halfway through this part of the journey. Please continue to pray that God will be with me and that my healing will be complete, In Jesus Name. I love you all.

Mountain is Just a Hill
Apr 7, 2013 8:59am

In a few months I hope to look back on this time and be able to say, "What once looked like a mountain is just a hill, from Heaven's point of view."

That does not mean I am ready to die, by any means. But this last chemo round and then the shot of Neulasta to rebuild my white blood count have kicked my rear. I always have had enough pain to deal with but that shot makes every inch of me hurt in places I didn't even know I had. I know that God has a plan for me and that He is working it, and I am really trying to praise Him through this storm, because these chains that bind me now can only drop behind me when I praise HIM. I had no idea one tiny little shot could do this to a person. They explained that it forces my bone marrow to work and produce white blood cells. OKAY, and then let's get it over with. Now, they tell me I will get one after each two days of Chemo. Thankfully, I only have 3 more months of this before they start retesting for the Lymphoma. I expect it to be gone. They told me in the beginning it goes dormant but remains in the body. That's just not good enough. We have a big GOD, and I expect big things from HIM. I want this stuff eradicated.

Please don't be upset with me if you call and I am asleep through half of the conversation. I am having to take a lot of pain meds to deal with what the shot is doing, but they did say I will be better in a few days to a week. Thank God for that.

Problem is that my immunity is now completely gone because the white cell count dropped so low. This is just a step for a stepper.

My bird, Lady Blue, just said, "God Bless You." The music on is, "I will praise Him, I will praise Him, Praise the Lamb for sinners slain. Give Him glory all you people for His blood can wash away each stain."

Sounds like a good place to stop.

When I Survey
Apr 8, 2013 11:34am

When I survey the wondrous Cross, and all that it tells me about my Lord. When I survey the world around me, and all the creation that God has blessed us with, when I survey the trees, green grass, birds singing, and children playing... It all reminds me that God is still on His throne, and that all is right with His world as He planned it. Then I have to bow and sing and pray, "For the sake of knowing You, for the sake of all You bring, I surrender all to You, my Blessed Lord, I surrender all to You.

It is so easy to get caught up in how much pain, or how much the temperature is, or how much longer I have to go. I need to remind myself daily to surrender all to HIM and to allow Him to handle all the problems so that I can rest in His healing.

I need to give Him my heart, and all that is within, I need to lay it all down for the sake of HIM my King.

It's not always easy to do this, I had a very rough weekend, but it is easy to remember He is in charge and I have given Him all authority in my life.

I love you all and covet your prayers.

Do Not Fear for I am with thee
Apr 10, 2013 11:07am

Awesome Joe read a billboard sign to me a few minutes ago,

> "DON'T FEAR THE FUTURE
> I AM ALREADY THERE.
> GOD"

What a necessary reminder. How many times did the angels of the Lord appear in the Bible and they always said, "Do not be afraid." I have known from start to finish that God is with me and I am not alone on this journey.

It was wonderful to be reminded. Joe feels pretty helpless right now, so that helped him also.

That Chemo and shot last week really got me good. I have been pretty much in bed since, just getting up when it is absolutely necessary. I am not complaining, I know that God is working this entire matter out to please Himself, and I am okay with that. If you remember, all I said in the beginning was that I wanted to touch someone's life with my life and actions. I want God to get the glory.

I fully understand that I cannot have a testimony until I have been tested, and somewhere in the future I will be called on to help someone else in this boat. I thank God for making it work. I praise Him because He is my all in all, and without Him this would be much worse.

He Will Never Leave Me
Apr 11, 2013 8:49am

Deuteronomy 31:8 NIV says, "The Lord himself goes before you, and will be with you; He will never leave you nor forsake you." Do not be afraid. Do not be discouraged.

Hallelujah. While all others are busy and taking care of what is important to them we have this one assurance, God will never leave us alone, He will never forsake us. We can't do or say anything bad to make Him go away. All we ever need do is say His Name.

Sandra Lopez, one of my dear friends, wrote a song, "WHISPER JESUS". I love to hear her sing it. See if you think you are alone all you have to do is whisper His name. He will be there for you. He loves you. He will always hold you when you can't hold yourself.

For the past few weeks, even though others have come in and been here for me, I was in a lot of pain and just wanted to sleep. I would take my pain meds and go to sleep. The easiest way for me to sleep during the day is with my praise and worship music on, in the living room. That way if anyone comes, I don't miss them. I turn the music on early in the morning and the parakeet, Lady Blue, sings with it. I lie on the sofa, with April on my legs and just go to sleep. I may wake up in 30 minutes or an hour. When I start to wake up, I have a praise song in my mind, which always helps to remind me I am not alone in this battle.

Poor Awesome Joe, he has come into the house and found me asleep (What again?) and can't believe that the house is so peaceful, and we are all just enjoying the peace. Others come in and quickly see that while I don't feel just right April is always there taking care of me. She should be a service dog. She can predict my headaches, my fibromyalgia flare-ups, and now she knows when I need to stay down and rest. As soon as I am okay again, she is back to her favorite spot, daddy's pillow. Even that stinky, hyperactive, crazy cat has learned to just lie quietly and let me love on him. It's amazing. I believe this is because they can sense that God and His angels are watching over me and they want to be a part of it. This is how God has allowed me to fight this battle.

On the other hand, when I do have visitors, they all know to back off and let me visit, and then as soon as the visit is over they are right back to lying on top of me. April is a mess, she thinks if anyone is here they have to love on her, and sometimes I have to put her in the bedroom to keep her off of people, but she knows that as soon as they leave she can come right back to mama.

God sure has planned my life. I am in the perfect place, with the perfect companions to fight this battle. And with Him beside me I can't fail.

Patience
Apr 12, 2013 10:03am

Not my strongest virtue, patience. I want my healing, and I want it NOW! It is so easy to say that. It is so easy to believe that something must be wrong with yourself if that healing you prayed for didn't manifest itself immediately. But you see, even though I was raised in a Pentecostal background, I have learned that God has a reason and a perfect timing for everything. After all, He planned my life before I was born, I am created to bring Him glory, and He knows exactly how to make my life work best for that point.

A few weeks ago, a man walked into my house and grabbed my foot, the only thing that wasn't covered up with the blanket in the living room, and he said, "It's okay; you're healed now because I am here."

Big news flash! I did not get up and take my bed and walk away. I am still here. "I will be complete when the Holy Spirit has finished His work and not before. God must get the glory from this journey." I actually invited his arrogant self to leave and, well, to get engaged with the Holy Spirit before he comes back.

I knew that once they started the chemo there would be no going back. They don't retest until the chemo is done, or something else happens. I knew that, so I knew that any healing would not manifest itself until this chemo is finished. The doctor said 6 months of chemo and 2 years of maintenance just to make sure the dormant tumors do not return. I made the choice then, that I do not want dormant tumors staying in my body. I want them completely eradicated, GONE. I don't have time to stop every few months and make sure the tumors are still dead and I don't have room in my body for any dead tumors to float around. I want them gone. Get out of here, in Jesus Name.

It's okay to be Pentecostal, I believe in healing too. There is nothing wrong with believing as I do. But people who foolishly believe and teach that healing should always be instant are not actually educated in the Word of God. That is not what He promised. He didn't say we would always have sunshine and joy that we would never have pain. What He promised was that He would be with us for the journey. He promised that if we continue to praise Him, then He has no choice but to bless us, and in blessing us we accept His healing, His joy, His strength, His blessings are true every morning.

I am looking outside at the little birds flying around and eating at the bird feeder. The sunshine has broken through and the last few days are gone. Winter is over and spring hath sprung. I have 3 pairs of Cardinals and 2 of Blue jays that come each year, I love to watch them. Last year we had baby Cardinals coming in to eat. I wonder if they will return this year. If not, of course, the parents will give us more to enjoy. I want to go outside and work my plants and rose bed. I have sinus allergies and the doctor told me it would be hard for me to fight a sinus infection right now, but soon this journey will be over. I have 3 to 4 more months.

Patience is not my best virtue. But I have His promises to carry me. I have His strength and His joy. Praise God, I have everything I need for the journey. Hebrews 6:15

KJV says, 'After he had patiently endured, he obtained the promise.' (That's what I want them to say about me).

Hebrews 10:36 KJV says, 'For ye have need of patience, that, after you have done the will of God, you might receive the promise.'

As you pray for me, pray for my patience, that I may endure so as to obtain the promise. My promise, my healing, my Lord: how do I separate them? He is my all in all.

My Destiny is Here with Me
Apr 13, 2013 9:05am

Destiny will be 13 in June. She called me this week and asked if she could come out this weekend and help me and visit with me for the weekend. I love this child, she is my special angel, and I have waited with great anticipation for her to come. It is a good thing that Joe is not here, because Destiny always shares our room, and she is the only one who gets to sleep in the room in my bed with me. No other grandchild has ever had that privilege. When her parents were breaking her to sleep by herself and I would be there for whatever reason, she would sneak out of her room and come to me and curl up with me. Her mama would come get her, wake her up, and take her, crying, back to the other room... saying she did not want Destiny to sleep in the bed with anyone anymore. I finally had to put my foot down and say, "I am not just anyone, I am grandma and I am not always here. Destiny knows that when I leave she has to go back to her room." End of story.

Now, when she talks to Awesome Joe and tells him she is here, he tells her not to sleep in his bed, and she tells him not to come home. But then, if he is home, she has no problem sleeping somewhere else. It is just something between her and me, and I figure when she decides she is too big to sleep in grandma's bed she will move. Right now, it is something special between us, and I treasure the memories. Today we are going to spend some quality time together, even though I can't get out much, she has come to me.

I am praying every day that God will use me to glorify Himself.

In view of God's mercy, I offer my body as a living sacrifice, holy and pleasing unto God, this is my spiritual act of worship. It is not in my own strength for it is you, Lord, who is all the while effectually at work in me, energizing and creating in me the power and desire, both to will and to work for your good pleasure and satisfaction and delight. I can only say thank you for using and choosing me. Thank you, Lord, in Jesus Name.

I desire Healing
Apr 14, 2013 10:35am

Father, in the Name of Jesus I come before You now, asking you to heal me. It is written that the prayer of faith will save the sick, and the Lord will raise him up. And if I have committed sins they will be forgiven, (and I ask you for that right now). I let go of all un-forgiveness, resentment, anger and bad feelings toward anyone.

My body is the temple of the Holy Spirit, and I desire to be in good health. I seek truth that will make me free, both spiritual and natural, (good eating habits, medications as necessary, and appropriate rest and exercise). You bought me at a price, and I desire to glorify You in my Spirit and body, they both belong to you. AMEN

I had a rather rough day yesterday, and I slept many hours last night due to fatigue, but I believe it is God's Spirit watching over me and telling me when I need rest for the body to heal. I truly believe He is giving me wisdom in this situation and my healing depends on my submission to what the Spirit leads me to. That means when I feel bad, I am obedient and go to bed. No matter how long it takes, My Father knows what my body needs to recover from this terrible journey He has allowed me to go on. The only way I win is to be submissive to His leading, and so I am.

I do not believe God gave me this Lymphoma, I believe it is a destructive thing sent by Satan himself to test me. But I do believe that God will walk the journey with and for me if I am submissive to Him, if I praise Him enough, and if I allow Him to. After all, what is a testimony without a test? How could I possibly help someone else if I have never been there? I believe everything we go through is for our enlightening, so that we may more easily help others. I am here, Lord, use me. Let me grow in your wisdom, and in your truth, and let me learn something here that I can use to help others later.

I can fight this, I am going to win this battle because Jesus Christ already won it, I just have to remember to let Him do the fighting for me. I am victorious because of Whom I believe in. AMEN

Bless me Indeed
Apr 15, 2013 8:24am

Father, I have long loved the passage in Deuteronomy 28: 1-14 which proclaims your provisional blessings upon me and my family. I know for a fact that we are each and every one a descendant of Abraham once we have come to know you. Therefore, the blood covenant you made with him, you made with me. When Jesus died on the cross, He became my blood sacrifice. He finalized my covenant with you. You said even the fruit of my body would be blessed so long as I love you and follow your command.

I do love you, Lord, and I have tried to do as you command. I have given you complete control of my life. In so many ways, I can count your blessings every day, and I remember your covenant with me.

This healing which I seek to manifest, is a part of that covenant, and I thank you for it. We have a covenant and Your Word is true and you cannot lie.

I thank you for allowing me the freedom to simply praise you and walk in obedience to Your Word so that You can work in me. Amen

I spent yesterday afternoon with my parents, Leon and Ida Pickens. I curled up on the recliner and tried really hard not to fall asleep. We watched the movie Parental Guidance. How funny. Then my grandson came back to get me and brought me home. It was a really good day, and I wouldn't take for it. We had chicken strips, fried okra and macaroni and cheese for lunch. I have not been to my mom's home since I was diagnosed with this Lymphoma. Thank you. Lord for making a way.

My mom will be 79 in August. I can't spend enough time with her for me.

Awesome Joe is on his way home again and will be here (hopefully) sometime tomorrow. I believe he is going to stay with me for a few days. That would be so nice. I miss him when he is gone, and after all, tomorrow is my birthday, so I want to spend a few days with him.

God bless you.

We Magnify You, Lord
Apr 16, 2013 10:16am

Jesus, Holy One, Jesus, Deliverer, Healer, Great I Am, we glorify the Lamb.

I am having a birthday, what a great celebration. After you receive this diagnosis the first thing you want to do is ask how long? How long do I have? I did not speak those words. I did not let them pass my lips. I simply said to the doctor, "I sure am glad you didn't write my life story. Cause only God can do that."

He was rather surprised, but then decided I was serious. Only my Father knows my days. Only my Father knows how many hairs are on my head. I have been walking this journey for 3 months now and I still believe only God has the answers.

I found out yesterday they are ready to do another test; I go in for a CT scan on the 24th. It will be interesting to know the results of this scan, because after the initial diagnosis this was how they measured the prognosis. Remember my prayer is that they will find the tumors gone completely. They said that does not happen, but they don't know what God can do for me.

I refuse to give in, and I won't give up. No matter what they find, this is God's work and it is continually in progress. I am expecting Him to do 'EXCEEDINGLY, ABUNDANTLY ABOVE ALL THAT I CAN ASK OR THINK.' No matter what, they will see the glory of God.

What a great way to celebrate a birthday.

What a wonderful day
Apr 17, 2013 12:41pm

Yesterday was my birthday, and a wonderful day it was. It started Sunday with a day with my Mom and Pop, then on to Monday afternoon when the messages started coming in. Yesterday, on my Facebook, I got about 35 messages and wall posts telling me happy birthday.

Awesome Joe woke me up at 8 am calling to say Happy Birthday, and as I was hanging up with him my mother called. Then I started checking the computer. Wow. How can I describe the feelings? I can't.

When they diagnosed me with this Lymphoma, I knew my life would change forever. I knew without doubt, that anything could cause me to flash. What hit me in the face yesterday was this... If the doctors were right, then I might not have many more. I didn't dwell on that thought, I rebuked it and went on with my day. I plan to be here, until Jesus calls me home, and He can do that anytime. It's just that simple things can set your mind off.

We went to dinner after Joe got home, and then we came home and ate cake and ice cream. Then my poor hubby got sick and was up and down most of the night. He seems to be better this morning, and he is planning to be here all week and I may be quiet.

I heard a song last night, on Sirius' southern gospel channel, Enlighten, and the words stayed with me, as long

I AM A VICTIM OF AMAZING GRACE

as there's a sea I have to cross, He'll move the waters for me. I didn't hear the title of the song, it was a men's group and that line was repeated a few times, so I think it was the Chorus. If anyone hears it, please let me know who it is. I loved the song, and it spoke to me.

See, God has been moving waters for me all my life, and I expect He will continue to do so. I have full faith in Him.

I love you all. God bless you.

CHAPTER TEN

During April 2013, America was struck by two terrible events. First, two brothers who were radical Islamists set off bombs in backpacks at the Boston Marathon finish line. So many people were killed or lost limbs; injuries were very serious. We haven't had a terrorist attack on our soil since September 11, 2001. It was indeed devastating, and I was one who watched the story closely. I prayed for the survivors; I prayed for the bombers, that God would forgive them, and I prayed for America. We are a nation at war with an unseen, undetected enemy and our leaders need wisdom and strength to deal with this. Second, just a few hundred miles away from my home, an explosion took out half of the town. People were killed and injured, school buildings and homes completely destroyed. What a tragedy! The State of Texas, my home, has never seen such an event so up close and personal. The people were devastated, 19 firemen and first responders lost their lives that day. How you comfort a town of 800 or 900 people, especially when those 19 were mostly local boys, belonging to local families? Every single family in that town was affected.

How could I ever complain about a little bit of pain? How can anyone complain about the simple things when others are going through so much?

It is our responsibility, as Christians, to help out as much as we can. We should be able to put our own situations aside and help with food, housing, clothing and anything else these people need. Too many of us are tempted to sit around and complain about our lives. We often allow ourselves to think someone else will help. But, if we are Christians then we must do everything we feel led to do to help.

Before you start thinking up excuses, let me remind you that Jesus Christ did not have any qualms or excuses. He could have called every angel from Heaven to help Him off that cross. He could have spoken the word and been released immediately. Yet, the only time we saw him ask for lenience was in the garden where He prayed, 'Father, if it be thy will, let this cup pass from me.' He didn't stop the crucifixion because He knew that we needed Him. He was our blood sacrifice, our redemption from a sinful world into which we are born. All He asks of us is that we help our fellow man in times of need.

I was totally unable to leave the house; I couldn't go and lend assistance. So, I prayed. I prayed, and prayed, and then I prayed some more. If it is all you have then God himself will make it be enough.

God only wants our obedience, our submission to His will, and then He can multiply nothing but prayer into something huge. He honors the spoken word from our mouth. If you really want to see Him at work, begin quoting His own Word back to Him. Scripture tells us that His Word accomplishes that which it is sent to Isaiah 55:11, and that the spoken Word gets His attention faster than anything else.

I like to have praise meetings. We just call our friends up and say, 'Do you want to come for praise?' They come. I have had as many as 20 people in my living room, and as few as 2 or 3. We turn the praise music up, we don't bring the negative, personal conversations are not allowed in the area where we are praising God. Take it outside. We have praised God for as little as an hour or as long as the night in dead of winter. People have arrived at my house around five or six in the evening and left at eight o'clock the next morning. The only rules we have are simple: bring your prayer requests written down (and I provide paper and pen for those who think of something), leave your personal problems at home and no personal conversation in the prayer room. We minister to each other. We praise the Lord. We pray over the paper stack. When we feel like it is over, everyone goes home. I don't care if they stay thirty minutes or all night. Nothing matters except that we praise the Lord.

I started a list of the prayer requests in the beginning and we were all amazed when, just a few weeks later, we were able to scratch things off the list. It was awesome. We weren't necessarily talking about the requests. We were just praying over a stack of papers with requests written on them. Believe me when I say, it was fun marking items off the list. We saw families restored. We saw babies come forth when the doctor said there was no way she could have one. We saw men and women with better jobs than they ever had before. We saw teenagers turn from drugs and alcohol to being soul-winners. I am telling you there is nothing more powerful than praise and the spoken Word of God.

A lady by the name of Barbara Arbo came to my church one time to teach a women's retreat. She was there for two or three days. One of the lessons she taught was that there is a Scripture for every single situation you can face. She told us a few of her own examples, such as child birth and a verse in Psalm that says He will enlarge you in your distress. I don't remember the others specifically. It has been at least twenty years since she came and I attended. But I remember that example and have used it many times when children are being born.

If you speak the Word aloud, it cannot return to you void. God's promise is that if we speak His Word, He will cause His Words to come alive inside us, and the Word will accomplish what it is sent to (Isaiah 55:11).

I used to tell my nieces and nephews who would say they were scared of the dark that there was a scripture for that. 'God is my helper, I am not afraid.' I would teach them to repeat it every night. I taught them to say it if they woke up afraid, or if they had nightmares. Without fail, every one of them was changed. They stopped being afraid. They were speaking the Word of God into their situation.

Even when I have a bad day and my son and I do not agree on everything, which can be often, I remember to proclaim Deuteronomy 28 over him. 'Even the fruit of my body shall be blessed.' And he is. He is blessed with five children who love him; he has a wife who would do anything for him. And he has me and my Awesome Joe. He has a pacemaker to keep his heart beating. He has his life, which the enemy tried to steal. He is happy and content with his life.

His oldest son is twenty-two years old, and I use the same verse. 'Even the fruit of my body shall be blessed.' He is my seed. He passed through my blood in his father. I claim the Blessings of Abraham for him and for all the grandchildren. I don't care if anyone thinks I am stupid or that I use scripture too much. I just keep doing it. I may be a fanatic, but at least I am a fanatic for Jesus, not for drugs or rock music.

When I had the little bookstore in town, the Lord blessed me with a spirit of laughter. It lasted for about a month. Everywhere we went, I would start laughing. I was so full of joy. The laughter would just roll from somewhere inside me and I could not turn it off. My husband told our friends we couldn't go anywhere right then because I was subject to laughter at the drop of a hat. We went to a southern gospel singing one night, and I started laughing, it was rolling up from somewhere deep inside me. I could not stop. He led me out of the building and said I had to stop. I couldn't stop it. I was so happy. I was full of Jesus. I was fasting and praying and laughing. (It was a good thing that was a Pentecostal singing; otherwise they might have called the looney bin for me.)

We must begin to program ourselves to speak with joy, and with certainty about everything we face. I could have cried over the diagnosis of Follicular Non-Hodgkin's Lymphoma. I could have done many things. But nothing would have brought glory to Him except my praising Him. And remember, I stood back and let Him take over. I let the praises roll. It's really the only thing to do when you need a miracle. I let the praises take over. And I got the miracle I needed.

Did you miss me?
Apr 19, 2013 9:15am

Sorry, guys, yesterday was a bad day and I spent it sleeping. Sometimes it goes that way. Can't complain though, April kept me company, Pooh Bear decided to knock my feet off the sofa since he couldn't eat them, and Lady Blue (the Parakeet) sang to me all day. Awesome Joe was in and out and checked on me often. That's a good day in my book. Corey and Sandra came in about 6 this evening and asked how I was doing; I was able to tell them that Joe had taken care of me all day long. He is good to me.

Now, otherwise, how could I complain with all that is going on in Boston and West, Texas? So many people have lost so much. So many have been injured or lost their lives and loved ones. How can I complain? I really do want to emphasize that we have no room for complaints. We should be praying for these communities, these people and doing all we can to help.

No, I don't feel wonderful, but compared to these stories, I am great. God has been good to me. I am His child. I pray that each of these people who lost their lives knew Him. I pray God's mercy on these terrorists. I pray God would forgive our sins and heal our land. I can't be the only one praying it though or it may never work. We all have to pray this.

My healing is secondary and not important compared to this. Our nation needs a healing, from top to bottom. It doesn't matter who is in power or who lives in the White House. The only thing that matters is that we get God back into America and that we turn back to our Creator, for forgiveness and healing.

I do feel better today, and I am going to try to spend the day with Joe, not sure how long I can go, but just a few hours are all I need.

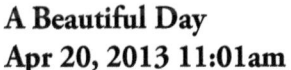

A Beautiful Day
Apr 20, 2013 11:01am

Yesterday was a beautiful day with my hubby. I rested yesterday morning, so we could go to Tyler last night.

Now, I know you don't want to hear it... but we started with an early dinner at the Texas Roadhouse, where we enjoyed Filet mignon with salad and baked sweet potato. It's been so long since we were there, I sat and held that steak in my mouth and just enjoyed the flavor. After dinner, I was already tired, but we had to go over to the mall and get my jewelry cleaned and inspected, supposed to do that every 6 months and it has been almost a year. Next, we went into JCPenney's and I got myself some new slacks to wear. It was time because I was down to 2 pair. I hate going when I can't take the time I want to shop. I tried on one pair and realized that was the end of me. These heavy sweats I get just don't allow for someone else to need something. I should have ordered them online, but they wouldn't have fit. Joe has needed a new wallet, so I told him he had better get it while I was busy, because I was tired and ready to not go into the store, only necessity drove me. It took him longer to pick out one wallet than for me to pick up 4 pairs of pants and 2 pajamas.

Today, I have to rest again, because that wore me out. Tomorrow we are going to church. Look out Barn Fellowship, we are both coming.

I didn't tell you that Corey came up Wednesday and changed the dressing on my PICC line. He did a great job, and I think he could be a pro in a few years, if he ever settles down and decides what to do with his life. He listened to me and did it slowly and carefully so as not to hurt me. He is great about helping me with this. And he and Sandra help me with meals and stuff. If I ever call them and say I can't do it, they are right here. What a blessing they are in that area. They do all my shopping for me, and I don't usually have to get out. I love those two kids so much.

God has been so good to me, where do I start? I can't even begin. But tomorrow, I will try. I know there are more bad days than good right at this time, but I know that God is healing me from the inside out. When He is finished, this body will be perfect, but I hope that's a time away.
I love you all.

Church at Barn Fellowship
Apr 21, 2013 4:54pm

Well, with Awesome Joe home, we went to church this morning. It was pretty wonderful. I love my church family, and I love being with them. I really miss them when I can't go, but sometimes I just don't have the strength to do it for myself.

This morning was truly wonderful. The music was great, the preaching was out of this world, and at the end of the service they had the women gather around me and lay hands on me, while the men laid hands on Tommy. Tommy is having a procedure done to his shoulder on Wednesday. They prayed for both of us. I cried unashamedly and felt totally comfortable just letting the Lord wash me with His love and I knew we were touching Heaven. For that, I am most thankful.

Sometimes it is hard to be honest with those who ask me how I am doing. If I say I am fine, then you expect me to be up and about, doing everything I normally did. I don't want to be dishonest, but I do want everyone to understand that when you are walking in faith, you don't speak the bad. I try to keep that to myself. Poor Joe has seen a lot of surprises this week, he has not been home in several weeks except for the one day a week. This week he has watched me for several days, and the changes are evident.

Please understand that if I say I am fine, I am speaking in Jesus Name, and trusting Him, and not living in my words.

I love you all. Please sign my guestbook.

I AM is there
By Ida Helton — Apr 22, 2013 11:28am

Awesome Joe was driving in across west Texas on I10 a few weeks ago and he read the billboard to me. "Don't fear the Future, I AM already there." signed by God. Wow, nothing to fear but fear itself. He is already there. Nothing they can do to me, so long as He is already there, that can scare me.

I have been so blessed the past few months to be able to share my thoughts and hopes. I am very blessed to have the best family to support me and the best church family to stand with me and keep me covered in prayer. Sometimes we forget I am supposed to be sick and I just push too hard to do other things. This last week, Joe came in on Tuesday night, and I wanted to spend time with him. We did what we normally do while he is home. Go, Go, Go. He never stops. The man is a virtual machine and he just never stops.

I told him Saturday, I was really tired. He said we could rest on Sunday. HAHA. I rested. He went. I came home from church and made us a couple of salads. Then I went to sleep for 4 hours. He woke me to say he was going to Dallas to take the trailer in. When he got home I was in bed. I slept all night. He woke me up at 9 this morning, guess he had been up for a while. He asked me if I was going to wake up. I said, "Yes, when I wake up." He thought that was funny, turned his back and left the room. Stinker came in the kitchen and made himself cereal and toast and didn't make me any. He ate without me, and then he got in the vehicle and left again. GO, go, go. He can't stop.

Corey and Sandra are out looking for work, both needing jobs. I am in the house by myself, thought I would make chicken noodle soup for tonight. It smells good, but now I am hungry and no one to fix me anything to eat. Wah. Guess cereal and toast will work for me too, but I have to make the effort to get it myself. I am really trying to eat wisely this week, more so than normal, because they check my weight every time I go to the doctor, and I want them to see the real me.

Those steroids they give me make me eat and balloon.

The truth is I feel fine today, just a little tired. Probably rest again this afternoon. Can't afford to let this catch me. I am trying to let God do His work, and that means I must do as He says.

If I tell my husband I don't feel like cooking, wonder if he would take me back to the Roadhouse to eat. No, not seriously, but he really does not like to cook. He would rather go pick up a sandwich or burger somewhere than come in the kitchen. Well, tonight we have soup. Tomorrow he will be getting ready to leave again. Our week is up and it is time for him to leave again. I can tell you now, I will probably cry when he goes. I love that man so much, and I hate to think of him out there all alone, and me stuck here.

I love you all, thank you Miss Vivian for your words of encouragement. It really is hard sometime to know what to say. You helped me with that one. I love you. See you soon.

Please sign my book, it tells me you are here. Are you WITH Jesus

By Ida Helton — Apr 23, 2013 1:21pm

My favorite Facebook quote today:
YOU ARE SAFER WITH GOD IN THE MIDDLE OF A STORM THAN YOU ARE ANYWHERE ELSE WITHOUT HIM.

I am so glad I know Him. I am so happy I can say I can't do this without HIM. He is my daily bread, my air to breathe, His Word spoken to me is all I need. I am desperate for HIM, and I would be totally lost without HIM. I am even happier to say I am not the only one who feels this way.

One of the pictures that stood out to me during the coverage of the Boston bombing was a lady who had dropped to her knees and began to pray, immediately the bombs started to detonate. She didn't run for safety. She didn't turn away. She fell to her knees and began to pray to the Father in Heaven, in that moment He was her counselor and friend, her keeper and her shepherd, and she committed her life to Him to pray for the safety of others. That stood out to me, because she stayed right in the danger zone. She did not hesitate to begin to pray. How many of us can do that?

Today, Awesome Joe and I ate breakfast at Denny's (I am sure thankful for all those coupons they sent out) and the first thing I noticed was that the party seated next to us was praying over their meal. Now, we do that at all times, but I am not used to seeing a lot of other people do it. Traveling over the country in a truck, I can honestly say we have seen a few people become angry because we had the audacity to pray in public. We had one couple who refused to eat next to us because we prayed. The server asked them if we had been overly loud, 'no' were they intrusive into your meal, 'no', did they disrupt your conversation, 'no'. She told them we had as much right to pray quietly over our meal as they did to leave. We have seen it all.

It moves me in my soul to hear people pray, even quietly, over their meal. I told the man at Denny's this morning thank you, and he told me he blessed everyone around him when he prayed. WOW.

He prays God's blessing on everyone around him. Isn't that awesome? Now, Joe and I never fail to pray over our meal, but this man actually said he prays for all those around him at that time. Makes me feel small.

I see so many requests to pray for someone or other who has cancer or some other dreaded disease. How can we refuse? We know that God is merciful, and He forgives the sinner and heals the body. I want to be the person who blesses all those around me. I do not want to be the one to hurt others or to ever forget that many people have it much harder than I do.

God has blessed me so much that when I have the bad days, I actually can sleep through them, not be sick and all as others are. I long for the day when cancer is eradicated from the world, when there is a total cure, but I fear that will never happen until Christ returns for His own. In the meantime, God please help me to remember to pray for others who may be in this position, or to minister to someone else that He is the only True Answer. He is the only one who can take the pain away. Thank you, Jesus, for just loving me enough, trusting me enough to let me go through this as a witness to you.

Lovely Day
By Ida Helton — Apr 25, 2013 8:22am

Yesterday I was quiet. I had to get up pretty early and go to Tyler for a CT Scan. Took us quite a while. By the time I got back I was tired and laid down and slept for about 2 hours. Then I had to get Corey and Sandra up here to help me move all the furniture and get ready for the cleaners to come this morning. Joe walked into the house with fifth wheel grease on his shoes last week, and I know better than to think I can clean it up. He usually walks from the shop to the house, this time he had jumped on the riding mower and came up. The grass didn't have a chance to clean his shoes and he didn't notice the glob on them. I just shrugged it off and said, I will call Ter-Jan as soon as you leave. He laughed and said we were due for a good cleaning anyway. That's the life of a truck driver's wife. HAHA

Anyway, today I am up very early because I am expecting the cleaners to be here at any time. I can't get into the kitchen because it is packed with recliners and sofa and tables and even an organ. Corey made sure I can just get to the fridge, so I can get ice and water. I have to drink about 3/4 of gallon a day because of the chemo. He left me a trail.

The cat is going crazy because he can't get to his resting place on the sofa. He keeps trying to get on the stove top. He's going to get in trouble in a minute. I wish I could turn the burner on, he wouldn't do that twice. Everyone is under orders to leave their shoes at the front door today, because you can't walk on wet carpet with shoes. They can't come through the back door, because it's a fire hazard right now.

When the carpet is dry we will get it all back in place and everything will look so much better.

I just saw my beautiful Blue Jay out on the feeder. The cardinals have already been here for a while. I love the Blue Jay, because when he shows up the cold weather is really gone.

I feel much better this morning and hope it will last all day.

All of you remember, you can't outrun God. You can't change His plans for you. He is almighty. He never forgets His plans nor His calling on your life. He will find you, and He will seek you out, and He will care for you as a new-born baby to perform His will in your life. He loves you, and His plans are good. My son told me yesterday that he is moving to northeast Oklahoma on the first of May. I am excited about that because he needs to be in a place where God can use him, and where he and his family will be available for God's purpose. I will miss him. Corey said, of course, how will we visit him, and my best answer is we won't be able to go. He will be living 5 to 6 hours away. But I know God's will is working in my son's life and I am pleased by it. I have long prayed that this would happen. Besides, away from other influences, he has work of a missionary to do, and that is Indian Territory up there.

I love you all. Have a great day.

I can't stop working while I wait.
By Ida Helton — Apr 26, 2013 9:24am

OFTEN THE ANSWER TO OUR PRAYER DOES NOT COME WHILE WE ARE ON OUR KNEES BUT WHILE WE'RE ON OUR FEET SERVING THE LORD AND SERVING THOSE AROUND US.

I could stay on my knees continually, I could live in this prayer that I will be healed instantly. I could dwell on it permanently until it comes, and I may be dwelling on it until the day I die.

I get up and go on. I don't ask Him every day for my healing. I answer the door and the phone, and I hand out food, I send Corey to the store to make sure there is food in the freezer for the food ministry. I do not fail to keep moving forward. Sure, I have days that I don't get dressed. I do have bad days. But I don't moan and groan about them either.

Bad days are the days you usually do not hear from me. My daddy always said, "If you can't say something good, don't say anything at all." He meant talking about people, but I took it pretty much to heart. If you complain all the time, people get tired of hearing it and move away from you.

But I strayed from my subject. There is a time to continually ask God for something. Jacob wrestled with the angels all night and told them he would not release them until they blessed him. Sometimes you just have to. But, usually, as an act of faith, you pray for something to know He has heard your prayers, you thank Him for the manifestation of the answer and you move away from the subject. After that, you should trust Him for the answer. I trust my Father completely.

Jehovah Jireh is my Provider, Yeshua is my Healer. I will walk this journey for His sake. Whatever comes, I know that He is in charge. He has promised me that so long as I take Him with me Everything will be all right. I live in that promise. He is my Peace. He is the reason I walk and talk and breathe. I know that at the end of this journey I will be a walking, talking testimony to His perfection. For that day I am ready.

I had two people call and come by yesterday for food from Eagles Landing Ministries. I used to deliver every time, but now I have them come to me, or Corey delivers the food. God continues to bless the ministry and people continue to be fed. This is my calling. To feed the hungry here. I can't stop on them. I have to keep working to get them fed.

Then, when God is ready to manifest His healing in me, I will be ready to step back into the helm and get back to full time work. Hallelujah. He didn't forget me because of the Lymphoma, He is using it to test me, and I pray that I pass the test. I just want to be able to witness His glory to these people who need Him so badly. Oh, and I had another call this morning, but they don't have the ability to cook, 3 children. I will take care of them for 5 days, until they get paid on the first.

My prayer for you today, is that you would recognize His calling on your life and live up to His test. Believe me; the rewards are out of this world. I love you all. Thanks for signing my guestbook. Makes me feel so loved.

Spring hath Sprung
By Ida Helton — Apr 27, 2013 1:02pm

I am so excited to see warm weather. It feels really good to know the cold is over. This is my favorite time of year. Cool enough to get outside, warm enough not to wear jackets. God must really have loved us to give us this beautiful time of year to watch as the flowers resurrect, and the green comes back to life in our world. The colors are so vibrant and the air smells so fresh.

God created a world full of color and sunshine. He created a peaceful place where He could come and walk in the garden and talk to mankind and be in communication with him. Thank God that He did. He really wanted someone to communicate with. He wanted someone to love and to love Him back, no matter what.

I think about my calls with Joe. Sometimes we are on the phone for a few hours. Sometimes our calls our quick. One night while we were having one of those long conversations one of our drivers was here. I had been silent for several minutes when he looked at me and said, "Are you still on the phone with Joe?" YES. He said, "But you haven't said a word in so long, I thought you were off." My explanation to him was that sometimes we do that. We can wait for minutes, just listening to the others breath or to what is going on in the background. It gives me comfort, and I hope it does Joe too, to know that he is there, waiting for me.

God is like that. We don't have to be in constant talk mode. He understands. He knows our quiet times. But He wants to be our companion while we are quiet. He wants to be the center of our world, the first thing we think about in good times and bad times. He does not want to be last place and He does not want to be there for the bad times only. As a matter of fact, when you stay in contact with Him and give Him a full-time position in your life, it makes it very easy to call His name first in the middle of an emergency.

One time, my mother and I were going from Terrell to Tyler. She was driving, the road was damp, and we were in very heavy traffic. just as we got near the old rest area that was around the 510 Mile Marker on I 20, we lost control. The car went right first, then left, and then off the road. No one hit us on the road. I remember calling out "Jesus" and my mom said, "God help us." The car came to rest about 100 ft down the median. We had a blown tire. As we climbed out of the car, we saw people running to help. One blown tire. We heard sirens. The highway patrolman who responded said he had a report that the car was flipping end over end. We didn't feel that. We never thought the car turned or anything. Amazing though, there were no tracks in the mud where the car had been. Just where it left the road and then where it came to rest. God is always there, and if we are in constant contact with Him, then He is free to help us without a long drawn out prayer in our time of emergency.

I didn't fall down and cry when they told me this diagnosis. I walked to the car, called Joe, and called Brother Jerry, my pastor. I just knew He was in charge and I could make it with Him on my side.

Today is a good day for me. I am resting so I can go to church tomorrow. I love you all and will talk to you tomorrow. Be blessed and continue to love the Lord for His mercies are good and He will always love you.

Sunday afternoon
By Ida Helton — Apr 28, 2013 2:33pm

It's Sunday, and I think it's a good afternoon to just lay around and watch tv. Lunch on the stove, be ready in a few minutes, and then I am going to rest. Hope you all enjoyed church this morning, I did. And then I know I won't be able to go back for 2 weeks, because I start Chemo again on Wednesday. I love you all. God bless you as you enjoy your day of rest.

This is Me
By Ida Helton — Apr 29, 2013 10:11am

In the battle, I batten the hatches. When the storms rage, I turn my face upward, because I know I can't face them on my own. When I get tired I simply ask Him for rest, and when I need peace I simply I ask for peace beyond human understanding. I know where to go for the answer.

When I was small my parents taught me that faith was believing that God would answer any and every need. They didn't say desires, or wants, because sometimes those don't line up with His Word they said. I have learned many things in my life.

Robert Schuller (Crystal Cathedral) said in a sermon one time that there were only three possible answers to prayer: yes, no, or wait. He said sometimes we get an immediate answer of yes, because we ask right and it aligns with the Father's will, sometimes we get No, because there is no way God would give us something that could hurt us, and sometimes we just have to wait until everything is right. The biggest testimonies come from the WAIT answers, because our faith must stay strong while we wait.

Psalm 37:3-5 NKJV, "Trust in the Lord and do good; Dwell in the land and feed on His faithfulness. Delight yourself also in the Lord, And He shall give you the desires of your heart. Commit your way to the Lord, trust also in Him, and He shall bring it to pass." Let me give you something to think about here. If we dwell with Him in the land, if we FEAST on His Word, then our will begins to conform to HIS. When this happens, His will becomes our desire. He is to put the desire into our hearts, because we have created fertile ground. Therefore, because the desire of our heart is being led by HIS WILL then when we ask, before we ask even, He is preparing us to accept the desires of our heart. And He gives them to us because they are His Will for us.

When you think about it, it's really pretty delightful. "He who dwells in the Secret Place of the Most High" (Psalm 91:1 NKJV) to dwell means to live, and to live means to be there continually. So, He is telling us to DWELL with Him, to transform our minds with His Word, to conform to His Will for us, then He is free to give us new desires. New desires will automatically line up with His Will for us. That is why He can so freely give us the desires of our heart.

For me, His will is for me to prosper and be in good health even as my soul prospers. Therefore, as my soul prospers, I will receive my healing. That is the basis for my faith in this situation. It's not what anyone has spoken to me verbally. It's not some dream. I have a Scripturally based belief that my Father wants to see me prosper and be in GOOD health. Lymphoma does not exist in GOOD health. Therefore, I believe He will heal me.

His answer to me was YES before the prayer was spoken. But it was qualified with a wait. Why I do not know. Not concerned. He told me in the beginning that if I would take Him with me everything would be okay, and it has been. I am so blessed I can hardly keep my socks on.

Wow, now I am tired. that took a lot. Love you and will talk later.

God is a Great God
By Ida Helton — May 2, 2013 4:09pm

My friend of olden days used to sing a song, God is a great God, and a Great God above all.

It is by His Grace and Glory that I am able to be here. He is the One who keeps me going and He is my strength. Today He has said rest is what I need, and today I shall rest. I am about to climb up in my recliner with some cover and relax for the next several hours. I thank Him for bringing me this far. Amen.

Lord I just rest in Your love
By Ida Helton — May 3, 2013 10:11am

I am resting in Him. The past two days have been pretty hard, but He is my strength. When I started this journey, others told me that the chemo treatments would get worse every time. They do. I slept most of the day Wednesday, yesterday was a day to sleep 2 or 3 hours and then get up and be awake for an hour or so. There is a LOT of pain in my right abdomen, where it has always hurt, and I have taken a lot of meds for that.

I go for that shot today, and then it's about 2 weeks before that eases up on me.

That's okay, God is healing me, and all this is going to be worth it in the end. God is healing me. God is healing me. He promised in the beginning if I would just be in obedience, He would use it to heal me, and He is healing me.

I am praising Him for all things, and I am getting ready to return to Tyler. Today my parents are going to take me. They jumped at the chance that we might be able to eat in Tyler when we finish. Thank God for parents who still care enough to be there for me even when it's hard for them.

I love you all.

Rough times are okay
By Ida Helton — May 5, 2013 8:01am

I had a hard time with the Chemo this last week and then got the SHOT on Friday which has created havoc in my body for the past 40 hours. I am sure glad I know that it comes to an end and that it has a purpose. That makes it all worthwhile.

God never promised me a rose garden, permanently filled with beautiful roses and no thorns. He didn't promise me that I would never have troubles. He didn't promise that I could just lay down and everything would be immediately all right. No. But what He did promise was that He will be there with me every step of the way. The past few days are the ones when I can see only one set of footsteps. Sometimes it's hard to feel Him carrying me, but I know He is. He promised, and I sure don't have the strength to do it on my own. He is my constant companion. He is my strength and my shield; and He alone can heal me and make me whole. Praise God.

"He who began a good work" (Philippians 1:6 NKJV) in me will surely see me through to the end.

Poor Awesome Joe though, has had very little attention. He can't get a word in because every time we start talking I started gagging. I sure hope today will be better. I took more nausea medicine yesterday than I have in the past 4 months. When it came it was bad. Maybe today I can talk to him. I miss him when we can't talk, and I know he worries about me. Sometimes it can't be helped.

I love you all. Not doing much today because still pretty weak and achy.

Back to Doctor I go
By Ida Helton — May 6, 2013 7:32pm

If you haven't heard from me it is because I am trying to beat this pain. Finally called Texas Oncology and was told will have to come back in and see the doctor before they can give me anything.

I covet your prayers right now. Thanks, and I love you all.

Migraine, not cancer related
By Ida Helton — May 7, 2013 3:07pm

The doctor ordered a cat scan which showed them no neurological damage or anything like that. It is not cancer related, or chemo related, unless it is a side effect. Doctor said it is a Bilateral Migraine. Simple. Now going to bed with migraine meds and will be better by morning.

Thank God it isn't more of this stuff. And Thank Him again, because He is my healer and my strength. He gives the doctors wisdom to treat me.

Better days today
By Ida Helton — May 8, 2013 2:41pm

Well, we had quite a weekend. I took the chemo Wednesday and Thursday, went back to Tyler on Friday afternoon to take a SHOT and then home to rest. WOW. Woke up Saturday with a headache from the other side of Mars or something. Now, I am prone to migraines, and I know how they are supposed to feel, and this was totally different. I felt like someone had my head in a vice grip and they were trying to remove the top inch or so of my skull. The SHOT causes bone pain so I thought, well... here we go. But nothing I had in my box seemed to work on it.

When I called the doctor Monday, they were not thrilled that they couldn't just send me hydrocodone and be done with it. That stuff makes me act like I've had a stroke. Okay. Awesome Joe arrived home late Monday night and woke up early to drive me to Tyler. They did blood work, they did physical workover, and then they ordered the CT scan of my head. I still had the headache. Finally, they came and called us back again. She said I had a BILATERAL Migraine. I never heard of that. She said it could be a reaction to the Chemo mixed with the tension of life and chemo. Whatever.

We got the migraine prescription from the pharmacy, the pain pills I had and the muscle relaxers and I went to sleep. What a total relief.

Today I am tired, and we have found a few sore spots, but the headache is GONE. Thank you, Lord.

I know I said I wouldn't complain, and I am really trying, but maybe this will help you know where I have been the past few days. It is by the Grace of God I made it through. There was a moment in the middle where I just wanted to give up on the whole thing, but I still have that sign on my wall. "You are going to want to give up... DON'T." I can't give up.

I have to remind myself that in the midst of this chaos I have already got quite a testimony. After all, the tumors are shrinking, and I am getting better. How arrogant of me to think I could do that and say all that I did without some kind of back lash. Well, it's true. I am getting better, in Jesus Name, and the tumors are shrinking. Praise God.

Now, too much time on the computer is not recommended today, so I will leave you for a while. I love you all. Please sign my guestbook.

Your Name IS EXALTED
By Ida Helton — May 9, 2013 11:43am

Your Power is shown throughout the earth, O Lord. I know we don't always do what we are supposed to, but He is always consistent, He always does what He has promised. He is Omniscient, He is all-knowing. He is God.

He created us, and He knows these bodies of ours intimately. He fully expects us to do our best to attend to the needs of the 'temple' He gave us to live in, and then He does the rest.

I see more and more people I know or connected to those I know with this diagnosis of cancer. There are so many variations and stages and types of treatments I don't even know how the doctors are keeping up with them. But I do know one thing for sure, and this is that God knows and has already taken care of them. He knew before the beginning of time what would come and that all of these diseases would be grouped together and called cancer. He has the answer. He is the only answer.

If you know anyone who has this problem, all I can say is encourage them to get to know what the Word of God has to say. We must begin to constantly speak the Word over this situation and to praise Almighty God for His power, for His promises, and that the work is already done.

Yes, I feel much better today.

What a Blessed Day
By Ida Helton — May 11, 2013 9:04am

Did you miss me yesterday? All I can say is that the migraine is still messing with my physique a little bit. Something in there is bothering me, not in my head right now, but in my stomach. Because of the migraine I had a lot of nausea and the lingering effects of that are not comfortable at this point. Sometimes easier to rest than try to deal with it. But as you know, I don't like to complain, so I just try to stay quiet.

I wanted to share something with you.
Jesus Calling by Sarah Young

"Transforming you is delightful to Me. Only I know the full measure of your capabilities, and I work ceaselessly to help you become all I created you to be." -Jesus Lives by Sarah Young, p. 210

> "For You are my lamp, O Lord; The Lord shall enlighten my darkness. For by You I can run against a troop; By my God I can leap over a wall" (2 Samuel 22:29-30 NKJV).

•Ida Helton Beautiful thought. He is delighting in transforming me. I will be all that He created me to be.

To me, this was precious. His delight is in transforming me. How does He do that? By my allowing it. I have to give Him permission. I have to open my mind, it is my responsibility to READ and to absorb His Word. It is my responsibility to stay in communication with Him. He is my lamp, but if I don't light it and refill the oil, then the light goes out. He is my strength. It says I can leap over a wall and run against a troop.

Cancer is my wall right now. All these treatments are the troops. And He says if I will continue to do my part, then He will do the rest.

Isn't that beautiful? He alone is transforming me. He is healing me.

I believe if I was a preacher I could get a sermon out of that verse. It is awesome to me, that God sends His promises on wings of internet when we can't get it any other way.

I love you all, have a great day.
Happy Mother's Day to all you beautiful Moms.

Blessed be the Lord God
By Ida Helton — May 12, 2013 10:11am

Blessed be the Lord God Almighty, who was and is and is to come. Blessed be the Lord God Almighty, Who Reigns forevermore.

Bless the Lord O My Soul, Bless the Lord, oh my soul, and all that is within me, Bless His Holy Name.

How can we not bless His Name on this glorious beautiful Mother's Day?

I am so thankful that my parents raised me in the fear and admonition of the Lord. I am proud to be the child of parents who thought it was more important to love each other than to be politically correct. I am proud to be the child of a mother who disciplined us with love and a firm hand. We did not have everything we wanted, but Mom and Dad made sure we had what we needed. We didn't have a telephone in the house until after we moved to Terrell and we all started getting married and moving off. I think it was 1971. One sister married, one off in college, and me planning to be married soon. We didn't have color tv, the old black and white was good enough for daddy. There were 7 of us kids and Mom and Dad in a 3-bedroom house, so we didn't have our own bedrooms, we had to share (such horror in today's world). We didn't get rides, we walked to school. As we got old enough, we went out and got jobs to keep us busy, but also to buy what we wanted for ourselves. We didn't go out to eat as a family, but after we started working, we figured out how to do that separately. I did housekeeping and babysitting from the age of 13 so I could have my drinks, and hosiery for my shoes. My brothers had newspaper routes from the time they could get on their bikes and ride them and balance. Daddy taught them how to manage the money they collected so they paid the paper bill before they got extras.

We grew up with family values, we love each other, we take care of each other. We grew up with the values that make us appreciate when we get small things. We all know it's the small things in life that count.

The most important thing they taught us was to love the Lord. I mean they taught us to get our bottoms out of bed and go to church. They taught us to participate in the service. They taught us to pray. They taught us to give when time came. My Mom and Dad were my faith builders.

The most important thing I can do today is to honor my Mother. I do. I honor and love my Mother with all my heart. I love you, Mom. When this journey is over for me, when I can get around again, I am taking you to Olive Garden and we are going to have our hearts content of pasta.

I love you, Mama. I thank God for you, and I pray that you will be here with me for many years to come.

How's that for funny
By Ida Helton — May 13, 2013 10:06am

My sister lives in Northern Michigan and she told me she had snow Friday and Saturday. I live here, in Texas, and we had 80 plus degrees those two days. I am amazed at how the Lord keeps us all apart, and how He controls the weather.

Joe and I have comprised a plan that we are hoping won't backfire on us. I am going to go with him for a week. Scary thought. He will be in tonight and tomorrow. I am going to try to climb into the truck. If that works, then we are going to plan on me going with him the next week, the

22 to the 27th or 28th. Have to be careful because I have to be in Chemo again on the 29th, and my arm has to be taken care of, but he has recognized the signs and says he has to get me out of here for at least a day or two. Cabin fever is hard enough, but I am going flat out crazy. He says I can stay in the truck and he will watch me carefully and make sure I get lots of rest. That means, he will take care of the dog most of the time. Only other question now, can I get rid of the lingering effects of the migraine from last week's reaction. If not, it's a no-go. Can't take the chance on a relapse.

God has been so good to me that I can't even begin to thank Him for all of it. He has been my mainstay and my strength, and He gave me Joe to help me here and when Joe can't be here, I have Corey and Sandra. Sandra has jumped in and helped with all kinds of projects. She loves to come in and just attack my dishes or anything else that is here. She loves to cook, and always makes sure to cook enough for me. This is part of God's provision for me at this time.

Today, I have a hornet's nest to deal with. Got a letter from the IRS that has to be answered today, then I have probably 3 loads of washing, and get Sandra to run the vacuum (it hurts me). By the time all of this is done, I should be worn completely out, and then my Awesome Joe will be home just after dark tonight.

I got a message from someone in the middle of the night asking me to pray about their marriage and relationship, that was my first priority.

I don't mind staying here so much, I have all the comforts. But what I do mind is missing the fellowship with my friends and family. I missed my mom yesterday (will try to see her today), and her card is still over there in my living room. I missed seeing my church family, because I woke up pretty sick to my stomach, and that hurt because I always want to say Happy Mother's Day to the Pastors Wife. Without her, he might not be so good to us. Awesome Joe is on the road, and so I didn't see him, but we talked on the phone a lot. My son, Dewayne, called and said it, from Oklahoma. Corey and Sandra came in and said it, but then they spent the day with Corey's other family in Wills Point. I am so glad he gets to be with them. His mother died when Corey was 22 months old, and so they help him to know who she was.

This is probably enough rambling for one morning. HAHA. Sorry, my thoughts are on the IRS document lying in front of me. Pray for me, that I answer all the questions correctly now, because you know those guys have no mercy.

Sandra. I love her. Hope she knows it.

My soul magnifies the Lord
By Ida Helton — May 14, 2013 5:26pm

Today is a beautiful day. I am with Awesome Joe, the kids are working on jobs, Dewayne is happy in Oklahoma, my brother got some good news from a doctor regarding his back pain. My soul doth magnify the Lord. He is great, He is awesome, He is more than marvelous, and He is Wonderful.

I am still having a small trouble with my digestion and all, but at least I can move around today. That is something to be thankful for.

Since Joe is home, I do not want to be on the computer too long but had to say I am feeling some better. Hope it lasts. Love you all.

Jeremiah 29:11
By Ida Helton — May 15, 2013 1:38pm

Well, it's funny, but I can never make plans with Awesome Joe. Jeremiah 29:11 NIV says, "I know the plans I have for you." Awesome Joe came in and spent the day with me yesterday, and it took him about an hour to decide he was not taking me in that truck at any cost while I am going through Chemo and have this PICC line in my arm. There was no discussion. He said no. He said if something happens to me, he cannot stop the truck to take care of me. End of that story. God knew He was not going to let me go.

That's the funny thing about making plans around here. I yielded myself a long time ago to whatever God had for me to do, and whenever I make plans, He is quick to laugh and remind me it is NOT going to go my way. I love it when He does that, but I can't help wondering if somewhere in the future I can actually plan to do something. I was told several months ago, by a trusted prayer partner, that they didn't feel God ever wanted me to get in the truck again. Maybe they were right. I give up on that.

Awesome Joe did say that after the PICC line is out, after they finish the chemo, then he would love to have me just ride with him some. I am okay with that.

I seem to be all right until I eat the first meal of the day, then something happens to my entire digestive system and I hurt and do weird things for the rest of the day. Not a good idea to be out of the house for long. But that is okay too, because it keeps me in the quiet and away from those GERMS my hubby is so afraid of. Hopefully the problem will ease up soon.

He loved my new living room furniture that my son and I worked out a deal for. He said the living room looks a lot bigger, so today I am working on the redo of the windows and walls to match. Can't wait to see the finished product and get the den arranged for family.

God is good to me and He has blessed me with all spiritual blessings, and He has also blessed me with the best husband a girl could ever ask for. I don't know if I could ever have earned this, but I sure am happy He thought I was worthy of my life. I can't think of anything I need more than to love my Lord and my husband and family.

I love you all, please have a blessed day, and remember, God heals, God has a plan for your life and it is good. God knows how to make you happy and how to give you peace that passes all understanding.

Pray about everything
By Ida Helton — May 16, 2013 1:02pm

Philippians 4:6-7 NLT, "Don't worry about anything; instead, pray about everything. Tell God your needs and don't forget to thank Him for His answers". If you do this you will experience God's peace, which is far more wonderful than the human mind can understand.

As silly as it sounds, there is nothing more precious to me than my animals and last week my poor cat hurt himself pretty badly. Not sure what happened, but he's been walking around with one paw in the air. I prayed for him, because he is just a cat, but he is mine. I put my hands on that leg and prayed for him. Awesome Joe and Corey tried to help him, and we weren't sure if we were doing any good. Then, just like we thought, yesterday morning he demanded to be let out of the house. He came back about 4 this morning. The leg and paw are still sore, but definitely a lot better than I ever thought they would be. Thank God.

That is wonderful news to me, because even April (who usually wants to fight him) has babied him. I am watching him heal as we speak.

I am healing inside out, and I can tell the difference in most of my body. Some of it is slow, but watching the cat reminds me that God cares and that sometimes we have to be patient and wait upon Him. There is a reason for me to be in this journey, and I must learn from it because I surely do not want to repeat it.

Thank you for supporting me in this. Your prayers are precious to me. I love you all.

Storms are Temporary
By Ida Helton — May 17, 2013 10:20am

We watched the other night as storms ripped through North Texas. We have seen the news clips of the destruction caused by these tornadoes. It's never fun, it is frightening and horrible to watch all of this, but to be in the middle of it is even worse, and I heard someone say yesterday that all he could do was pray for safety. 99% of these people are just thankful to be safe, and not worried about the material loss in that sense.

When they told me I had Stage 3 Lymphoma I prayed first and then gave the entire situation to my Father and walked forward in trust. No use looking back. This journey is a storm that I must walk through. I am thankful to be a testimony.

I read two things this morning which, when added together, say everything I feel.

1. Let not the opinions of man interfere with the directions given to you by God.
and
2. "Sometimes, God doesn't take us out of the storm... He simply gets us through it." Joel Osteen

I felt very strongly that God wanted me to take this direction of chemo and rest for the healing. I have followed His path, even to allowing Him to help me pick the doctor who would treat me. It is not always easy, but it is always the best path to take. His path is the one we have to follow.

I thank God that He is getting me through this storm. This journey has had many ups and downs and will continue to I am sure. But as long as God is in the lead position, I expect to come out on top.

Thanks. I love you all.

Good Morning, Lord, It's Me Again
By Ida Helton — May 18, 2013 9:40am

Depending on Him means that I must do my part by staying in complete, constant communication. In order to facilitate this, I wake up and say Good Morning, Lord every day.

Do you know how good it feels just to hear Him in the silence? Just to know that He is God and He is in charge, so I can relax? I also say, Good night, Lord, just before I go to sleep. He is my first and last communication.

Then, every time I consciously think about it I talk aloud to Him during the day. Sometimes it is as simple as I love you, or thank you, and sometimes it is a prayer for others or for whatever.

The main thing is to be in constant communication with Him. Do not forget that He is your Creator and Companion. When we are in constant communication with Him, then the small things that come up are just that, small, and the larger things in life are very easy to hand to Him immediately.

This is my take. When the bombings happened in Boston, they had a clip of one woman who fell to her knees right there and began to pray. That is the result of constant communication. She didn't think to run. Her first thought was to bring Him into the situation. Hallelujah. That is where God wants us to be with Him.

I feel better today. Much better. I think I will just stay inside and allow Dewayne and the others to get the yard work done, so that I can go to church in the morning. Not taking any chances after the week I have had. I know God is in charge, but I am tired of being so sick.

To those who are near, see you tomorrow, and to all others, please keep me in your prayers. I love you all

My Redeemer Lives
By Ida Helton — May 19, 2013 8:11am

Who taught the sun where to stand in the morning?
Who told the ocean, you can only come this far?
Who told the moon where to hide till evening?
I know my Redeemer lives.

He lives to tell this cancer just exactly what it can do to my body, and exactly when it has to be completely gone. It is up to me to stand strong enough to pass the test, and to turn it into a testimony.

I must admit that at this point the bad days are outweighing the good, but that is normal. God knows what is coming next and He seems to prepare me for each step.

I am blessed, because there have not been many surprises, since the first diagnosis. I started listening really quickly.

The doctor told me that with this particular type of chemo I probably wouldn't lose all my hair, but I see it is thinning out significantly. I didn't have much to start with. The good news is they say it comes back in thicker, and boy could I use that.

He also told me I would tire easily, boy was he right on that. I don't dare try to drive myself far because when I just drive to Canton I am toasted when we get home. I try to make sure I have someone with me just in case, and this is me. I used to drive the truck 10 or 11 hours at a time, daily. I love to just get in my car and drive to Memphis or to other places. I hope I get all that back when this is over. I really miss being able to take care of my people out here.

Anyway, today, I am up and ready to go to church. Taking my son with me for the first time in over 10 years to my church. I am so excited. I have really missed my son, but through prayer and faith, God has brought him back to me. I can trust God to take care of him and his family.

I love you all. Thank you for your prayers.

The Lord is my Refuge and Strength
By Ida Helton — May 20, 2013 11:39am

Psalm 91 KJV says, "He that dwelleth in the secret place of the Most High, shall abide under the shadow of the Almighty. I will say of the Lord, He is my refuge and my fortress: my God; in Him will I trust. ... There shall no evil befall thee, neither shall any plague come nigh thy dwelling. ... With long life will I satisfy him and show him my salvation.

Psalm 92 begins by stating, "It is a good thing to give thanks unto the Lord, and to sing praises unto thy Name, O Most High".

I can't help it. He has been good to me. I dwell in His secret place and He overshadows me with His protection and strength. He even causes His angels to stand round about me and protect me from all evil. I must give Him thanks for all the good I have received.

My healing is in line with his Word, which says, "No plague shall come nigh they dwelling". I am blessed to be called one of his children. I'm still resting and avoiding crowds, I am still trying to do all I can to make the situation better. I am not giving up. I am being obedient and submissive. I want to dwell with Him in His secret place, and when I am there no evil can touch me.

Thank you for taking this journey with me. I can truly say that I am, at this point, a VICTIM of AMAZING GRACE. I am not a victim of cancer, I am a survivor. I am not a victim of all the curses that came with the diagnosis. I am declaring healing for myself and for my family right now, in Jesus Name.

Maybe two more months and we can relax and begin the true healing process, because the chemo was supposed to take 6 months, I think he said he may have to extend it a few months because my immunity dropped so low that he had to drop the dosage, but even then, I am thankful for the journey. It will make me happy to be free when it gets here, and my testimony will be so much stronger.

I love you all. Be blessed.

He's Still God...
By Ida Helton — May 21, 2013 9:31am

In the midst of all the chaos, He is still God. They can't even begin to take Him out of the picture. On one of these pages I read where someone wrote, "Didn't God cause all these storms?" The answer is no. NO. He didn't cause them. He is there even in the midst of the storm. He is there, wherever we will allow Him to be. He can be carrying us, or standing right beside us, or walking hand in hand. He's still God and He promised never to leave us alone.

We don't know why we have to go through life with tragedy and sorrow. We honestly don't know what causes pain. I can't say with any certainty, any more than the doctor can, what caused the Lymphoma for which I am being treated. What I can say is, "God is still God."

He is still on His throne, He is still there waiting for daily communication with His precious children. He loves me. He calls me His own. God is still God, and I rely on Him for everything.

1 Corinthians 1:10 NIV

> "I appeal to you, brothers and sisters, in the name of our Lord Jesus Christ, that all of you agree with one another in what you say and that there be no divisions among you, but that you be perfectly united in mind and thought."

He is still God, and we need to agree on that, and be at peace with His resolution.

Cancer has to bow. Tornadoes may cause severe damage and destruction, but the Bible says that weeping endures for a moment. God is still God. Only God can provide the comfort which is so desperately needed at this time. One of the nurses in the Chemo Gallery said, "It's impossible to work here and not believe in God." He is still God.

I love you all. Thanks for your support during this time in our lives. It means so much.

I can do all things...

By Ida Helton — May 22, 2013 1:40pm

I can do all things through Christ who strengthens me. I can do all things through Christ who strengthens me. I can do all things through Christ who strengthens me (Philippians 4:13 NKJV).

> "I (me, myself) can (am fully able to) do all things (everything, no holds barred) through Christ (Jesus, my Redeemer and Companion and Friend) who strengthens me (He gives me the strength, whether emotional, physical, or psychological, or spiritual)" (Amplified Bible).

"Eye has not seen; no man can declare the things that God has prepared for those who love Him" (1 Corinthians 2:9). He has prepared for me a way to overcome, and I sure do need it now. 3 teenagers living in the house with Gmaw and Gmaw is feeling trapped by the mob. Seriously, I am not used to the noise and the racket, so I guess I have to pray hard to make it the next week or so until they get a house. That's okay. I am going to make it, and I love these kids, just not used to having them all around at once. Come on house.

Anyway, I think today calls for quiet, and for rest. I spent yesterday afternoon with Awesome Joe, and I even helped with supper, but I am very tired today. I must stay on top of my health. I have to keep remembering that, "I can do all things through Christ who strengthens me".

That's just God.
By Ida Helton — May 24, 2013 12:59pm

I can't believe I missed posting yesterday. I had so much going on, and couldn't get people to cooperate with me, my computer decided to take a dive and would not go online. I had people calling me for information and I couldn't do anything. Seems if the computer is fried the brain is fried with it.

This is saying something because when I started the chemo I had to acknowledge that one of the side effects of chemo is major confusion and I told the young lady that my husband would never recognize it, but he seems to think I am further out now than ever before. He even told his son if I was looking for something it may take a month or two before I remembered what I am looking for, much less where it is. And then he laughed.

God has richly blessed me this week with my grandchildren all being here, and I survived it. I love these kids and would give my life for any of them, but I won't complain about having a break. I am tired now. I have let the others do the cooking and cleaning as much as possible, but I got up and made breakfast this morning. That was fun, until right at the end when my strength gave out. I was ready to cry uncle and realized they were all outside. I had to finish the eggs myself. But then, they did the dishes and now I am relaxing again.

I can't believe how God has taken care of my household this past several months. It seems that every time a need arises, God has the answer, before I can even ask about it. It has been awesome to watch this all fall into place in His timing.

He doesn't show up late, but always right on time. That's just God doing what He does.

I love you all...

DON'T GIVE UP
By Ida Helton — May 24, 2013 1:23pm

About the time we are ready to give up
   JESUS comes alongside and whispers...
     "DON'T QUIT, KEEP GOING...
       JUST KEEP YOUR EYES ON ME.."
                 HE HAS NEVER FAILED
ME YET. AMEN

Energy Zappers
By Ida Helton — May 25, 2013 12:01pm

    Worry is a zapper. Anger is a zapper. Self-pity is a zapper. Anything that takes away your energy or distracts you from your joy is a zapper. I am trying to learn to turn loose of the zappers. I think I should carry around a fly swatter and just swat at those little zappers every time I know they are present. I don't need to waste energy right now. I need all of my energy concentrated on God and my health.

    I saw something on Facebook this morning that said,
     "DON'T USE YOUR ENERGY TO WORRY...
      USE YOUR ENERGY TO BELIEVE"

    Now this makes a lot of sense. because if the little zappers are taking your energy, then you become distracted and stop believing. We can't afford to stop believing, because God honors our faith, not our lack of it.

    Even if we become a little bit angry, we should try to calm it down as quickly as possible and stop the drama. That drama will zap your energy. That is Satan's plan... to zap your energy and cost you your faith needed for healing or for finances, or for whatever you actually need.

Don't give in to it. Don't let those zappers steal your joy. It isn't worth the pain. Tell those zappers to get out of your way, In Jesus Name. Only you can prevent the energy zappers. Just a play on words there.

I am not feeling too good today, kind of achy all over and sick stomach. I start chemo again on Wednesday the 29th, and of course the SHOT comes on Friday. Will need all the prayer I can get on this one. And I will not let any zappers stop me. I will not let any zappers stop me. I will not allow any zappers to come between me and my healing.

Ready for a Break.
By Ida Helton — May 26, 2013 9:11am

I am ready for a break. I have gone from 1 good day to 2 bad, all the way to 1 in 5. Yesterday I was sore and pokey, today I am just flat sick. I went to bed at 8 pm and got back up just before 5 am to take pain and nausea medicine. I don't want to be sick, I don't want to have to plan around it, it just happens. I try not to complain, but this one is really getting to me and I really need a break.

One of our friends sent me a little card with an angel pin on it. She is called the Cancer Angel. I put her where I can see her at all times. I seem to need that encouragement right now.

I know that God has placed His angels round about us, to protect us and to keep us, and I know that all I ever need to do is call out and He is already there. I know that without Him I can do absolutely nothing, but we can all use these little reminders at times.

I don't know what I would ever do without my family and friends who have supported me here. I love you all so very much. I need your prayers, and I feel them. I know that you all care, and that helps me make it day to day. I am blessed to have you all, and I pray that God will bless each of you in return.

I am just ready to go on a cruise and relax on a sunny deck beside the crystal-clear pool and soak up some sunshine. (Not that I have ever done it, but it sounds good right now.) What I would really like is to be able to go with my husband for a few weeks and not have to worry about this PICC line in my arm, or how to shower with it, or being sick from the treatments (because that would slow him down), I just want to be near him and be able to cuddle up and sleep with my arm around him.

The good news is, he should be home Wednesday evening, and then he won't leave again until the next Tuesday. I like that. The bad part of it is, I have chemo Wednesday, Thursday, and the SHOT on Friday. He would manage to be home on my worst weekend, and for that I am laughing out loud.

No church today but doesn't mean I am not going to spend time with my Father.

I love you all, be blessed.

Better day today
By Ida Helton — May 27, 2013 9:53am

I feel much better physically today. Yesterday was pretty hard on me, but that seems to have passed. I rested a lot.

It's Memorial Day today, what a day. I think of all the men and women lost in the battle to care for our freedoms, my own husband was in the military during the Korean War. My father was in the army post WWII, though I am not sure of the exact dates. My parents married in 1950, and daddy had only been home a short time. My brother-in-law was in Vietnam and came back a changed man. He ended up escorting one of his best friend's body back home and that was about the last straw for him. He went over the deep end completely after that.

There were others we knew that went, and some came back, and some didn't. Since then we have had many skirmishes to send our troops into, and some wars. We have lost many men and women on the battle fields trying to preserve freedom for all. I know sometimes it seems like an endless battle, and we hate the loss but, in the end, freedom will win. We must believe that. If freedom were not winning then why are so many people trying to become Americans, legally or illegally? Why do they want to live here if we are not the greatest nation on earth?

Against all of this, cancer seems so small. My illness seems so non-important. There are so many others who need prayer and help today. I can't think of anything to say about my own that would make a dent in this world.

God help those who are remembering the ones they lost today. Please help us to at all times remember why we are free and to always thank those who fight for us and for others freedom. Help us to always remember other's pain over our own, and to always put others first. Thank you for the freedoms you have given us in this great Nation of ours and for allowing us to help other nations who do not have the same freedoms as we do. Thank You, Lord for always answering our prayers.

Trust in God
By Ida Helton — May 28, 2013 11:52am

I had a friend who lived in Memphis, Barbara Brown, she would always tell me, "Don't fret about it. Whatever God has for you is for you and no one on earth or below it can change that." In fact, there is an old Spiritual I've heard many times that says, "What God has for me, it is for me."

This morning I saw a quote from Paula White on Facebook,

> "TRUST IN GOD -- Nothing can stand in the way of what He decides to bring to pass."

To this I say, "Amen." Because what God has for me is for me. You can't take away my blessing unless I give it to you, and I am not turning loose.

I start Chemo again tomorrow morning. 5th round for me. 2 days every 4 weeks, plus on the 3rd day I go back for the SHOT. I do not look forward to the chemo, because this past 4 weeks has been hard on me, but I step out in obedience and go because I want this healing. I want the testimony that God is working in me. I want to be able to stand before my church family and say, "This is what God has done." I believe if I stay strong in my faith I will see a glorious end to this mess, and that is what keeps me strong.

Thank you for your prayers, and for your support and love. They mean so much to me. Please sign my guestbook, I really need to know you are there. I love you all so much.

I am Thankful
By Ida Helton — May 30, 2013 9:47am

My chemo went very well yesterday, but the doctor was not too pleased with the fact I've had so much gastric problems this past 4 weeks. He changed my nausea medications for the next 5 days and said that should help, then he did an examination and said I need to get an EGD done. He has ordered that, and we will see what it shows. He said after the first week I should not have this problem hanging on with this particular chemo. I am thankful, and Awesome Joe is also, because we finally have a doctor who wants answers and not just to treat his problem and go on. So, soon we shall find the root of this pain. Thank God for that. It's been around way too long, and the doctor said yesterday if it was part of this cancer it should have stopped already.

I am also thankful because the big day is over, today is about an hour and tomorrow is just a shot (in and out). Awesome Joe is home so he will be taking me tomorrow, and he might just make church on Sunday. He may not let me out of the house, but maybe he can go by himself.

I am thankful for the rules he has imposed on me, because he has taken good care of me throughout this illness. It is because of Joe's rules for survival and healing here that I am actually able to say I have had no infections, and no added problems with this.

I am thankful because my son has found a house and they will be moving out during the next several days. They really need their own space and I like my quiet. Not used to having this kind of company for more than a few hours or overnight. That's funny for me, after being raised in such a large family.

I am thankful because Awesome Joe is making me some toast and I will be able to enjoy it, if the nausea medicine works.

I love you all and. will talk again soon. Thank you for your prayers and support.

Almost done with this episode.
By Ida Helton — May 31, 2013 10:25am

I love my hubby so much. He is home and I feel so much better when he is here. He is taking me to Tyler for the shot today, and then he will be here with me until Tuesday.

That is probably God's blessing to me this week. He comforts me just by being here with me. I am so blessed to have him. The Chemo has gone okay so far, but they tell me to give the shot a few hours and let them know immediately if it gets worse. I actually cooked the scrambled eggs for us this morning.

Can't believe this is #5 of 6 months of treatments. After the next treatments at the end of June there will be another round of tests, and then we will go back to the doctor to see where we stand. He has ordered this EGD (upper GI scope) to see what is going on in my upper abdomen, and that may require even more stuff, but I can wait. God is Good, He is always Good and that is what I cling to most of all. His mercies to me are everlasting. His amazing grace will carry me through all of this and into my future. I am just so glad they found all of this before it got worse. His timing is perfect.

Please sign my guestbook, I really need the encouragement.

Well, It's Saturday
By Ida Helton — Jun 1, 2013 4:31pm

Chemo Wednesday, Thursday, and the SHOT on Friday, have left me down and resting. I have, in fact, been asleep on the sofa most of the day. I hate having to take the pain meds, but at least he beat the nausea with the other medicine. I take that on tomorrow also, and then we shall see what Monday brings,

I thank the Lord that He has brought me this far, and that is what I expect from Him. He is always, always, always right beside me. Each time we go to the chemo my friend and I pray on the way that He will go in with us. He always does.

I am blessed to have friends who have supported me through this. I love you all.

Be of Good Cheer
By Ida Helton — Jun 2, 2013 11:00am

If I don't say too much, then maybe my smile will deceive everybody. No, actually I think I will just crash on the sofa. Rough day today, headache is getting worse all the time, and I took a migraine pill last night, don't want to take another today. But, I will if I have to.

God is good. Awesome Joe prepared my scrambled eggs with cheese and toast for breakfast, and I am almost certain he will make me a peanut butter sandwich in just a little while. He is taking good care of me. I am so blessed to have him.

I love you all. Have a blessed day.

You speak what you put in...
By Ida Helton — Jun 3, 2013 10:26am

Faith talkers input Faith Scriptures all the time. They ingest them, and then they digest them, and then they (if you will pardon me) regurgitate them. This makes perfect sense to me.

If you put cherry Kool-Aid in a gallon pitcher, and mix it up, you drink cherry Kool-Aid, and your tongue turns red.

Some people say, "You are what you eat." Now, if you have an illness such as Celiac disease, you cannot ingest gluten, because your body will not digest it properly and you become ill. If you have high cholesterol, or diabetes, you must be careful what you put in your mouth, because it eventually comes back out and makes you very ill. Diabetes patients are supposed to control their carbohydrate and sugar intake, because these things become sugar in the body and the pancreas cannot properly process them. You get the gist of my conversation, I hope.

There is one particular advertisement on television, a small girl standing beside her father who has hit a trash can with the car. He starts to talk about the problems, and she takes on an adult voice and says, "you have Allstate..." and she rattles the words off to him in entirety. You know what she watches and listens to. Take a child whose parents teach them prayer and politeness and you will have a child who speaks in prayer and is polite to others.

When my brother was here a few months ago, they all went out to a favorite spot for burgers. As their food was placed on the table, some of the others started to eat. Brayden, my 4 yr old great nephew, stopped them all and said, "we didn't pray." Then he bowed his head immediately and prayed. That child has been taught to pray.

Take another child who lives in a (perhaps) non-Christian home, where the language reminds you of a bar fight, and listen to how their language comes out. Totally different. Totally sad for them, but all they know to speak.

Therefore, it makes perfect sense, that if you input Scriptures you will output Scriptures when most needed.

Like me, saying to the doctor who just told me I have about 5 years to live, "I sure am glad that you didn't write my life story. My Father wrote it before I was ever born." Based on Jeremiah 29:11 NIV, "I know the plans I have for you."

He already knows. He knows what His plans for me are. No doctor or bullet or villain can change that. I can't be taken out early for anything. He already knows.

Hallelujah. He knows what His plans for me are. His angels are all around me and watch over me continually.

I am still weak this morning but moving a little more. Trying to spend the day with my honey as much as I can, although I can't leave the house. He will have to leave again tomorrow and I will miss him.

Father's Day is June 16th, He placed his order yesterday. Guess he thinks I am going to run to Walmart and get it, but he may get a surprise. Will have to take it one day at a time.

I love you all. Have a blessed day.

Blessed my socks off.
By Ida Helton — Jun 4, 2013 3:00pm

I don't know where to begin. I sure am glad it was Awesome Joe who opened the mailbox. I don't keep secrets very well, and I would have spoiled it trying to decide what to do. I had asked Corey a couple times to check the mail but for one reason or other we never got it done, either the key was at home, or they completely forgot.

So, yesterday, while I am still sitting at home and allowing Awesome Joe to take care of all the business he went to the post office and came home with a big surprise for me. Social Security had sent several pieces of mail. He came home and handed them to me one at a time.

When I got to the one that said I had been approved for disability and how much I will be getting per month, I started shouting and praising God. He just stood back, watching me. I couldn't read the letter because I was shaking too much. He finally said, "I guess you don't care about this envelope..." and he laid down the check for the first payment. I cried, I laughed, I shouted thank you to God, and I called my family to get in here and to dance for me. They did.

You see, when God does it, it is right, and it is right on time. We have had the concern, since we have no other drivers and Joe is our income, if something had happened to him we would lose it all. Now, we can schedule him off for a week every month, Every month, 3 weeks out, 1 home. He can do it now and we don't have to worry. God is good all the time and all the time God is good. He has answered our prayers in ways we never could have imagined.

This morning, I had to get up and go get my hair cut, then we went out to pick out the television I have wanted for 10 years. No more hand me downs, no more redneck, just a big, beautiful 46" Phillips Smart tv. Awesome Joe is still in shock. He can't believe he did that.

I am tired and fatigued and weak. but it's done. We are putting the scene together now.

Untitled
By Ida Helton — Jun 7, 2013 7:44pm

I can't begin to say what the last several days have been like for me. I have been torn between blessings and symptoms, and the symptoms seem to have won on Wednesday and Thursday and so this morning I went to the doctor. The Fibromyalgia won for a few days.

Awesome Joe has been here, or I wouldn't have made it. He even drove me to Tyler at 5:15 am so I could be there for an EGD by 6:30. We were done and on the way home before 9:30.

I have been really touchy this week, my body is sore and reeling from an episode of Fibromyalgia. And now to make it worse, they have to put me on a seven-day step down of steroids to break it up. But pain pills and muscle relaxers help a lot.

The good news is that I have been approved for disability. That means that the government has said I have this stuff and the lymphoma badly enough to say I will never be able to work again, which I don't like, but at least it answers the problem of what to do if something happens and Joe can no longer drive the truck, or if he needs a few weeks off. It is a very real answer to prayers prayed by many people in the past several years.

On Tuesday, Awesome Joe and I ventured out and bought a new television, and that was a lot of fun for both of us... (she said while laughing out loud). Now I haven't bought or shopped for a nice television for the living area of the house in over 30 years which was probably a mistake. I did help to pick out a small television for our bedroom, like 19 inches, and I watch it at night when he isn't here. It keeps me relaxed. So, on Tuesday we went out to locate the Flat Screen television of my dreams. I never dreamed my husband and I would have so much **ahem... fun buying a television. We ended up bringing home my choice, a Phillips 46-inch, Wireless Smart TV, (and I will tell you what that is soon). Joe left this morning, and Corey now has to educate me on using the television for all its worth. Incidentally, the VIZIO the same size but not a SMART was $50 more, so I think we got the best deal. Now to find a few shelves to put over it so I can have my trinkets back up, and Joe's picture of Connie Smith of course.

Anyway, God has blessed us so much this week and I wish I were free to talk about all of it, but right now, I just need to get back to resting, because I intend to be in church on Sunday morning, and the only way that is going to happen is for me to stay down all day tomorrow. Yuk....

I love you all.

Preparedness and Readiness
By Ida Helton — Jun 8, 2013 10:14am

There is a quote that I see from time to time. "Lack of planning on your part does not create an emergency on mine." I saw that yesterday and my mind roared.

It's actually very funny if you put your Scriptural, Christian life up against it. We are called upon to be ready at all times, to be prepared for His return. We are supposed to read the Word and to ingest it so that it is our instant answer to any problem spoken or felt, real or imaginary.

What happens when we aren't ready and prepared for what life throws at us? We get discouraged, we fall apart, we scream and cry because we didn't prepare ourselves for the emergencies that come.

I know people who look for a reason to fall apart because it brings them attention. I have never understood them. I always wanted to be the one who leads through and comes out on top. I really want my family, friends and acquaintances to see me living a testimony no matter what.

What I am trying to say is, even though they diagnosed me with Lymphoma I knew at that very moment that God was in charge and that I could trust Him with my life. I drew strength from the Spirit within me, and I try daily to help others with my strength. I know He will honor me because of it, and I know that He has only my best interest in His plan. Everything that happens to us is already written in the Book of our lives before we are born. The difference is some people choose to react differently.

Prepare yourselves by reading the Word and daily prayer time with Him. Be ready when He calls on you for an action. Draw on that Spirit for how you are to behave and react. Remember the entire World is watching you and you are the only Jesus many people will ever meet.

Church
By Ida Helton — Jun 9, 2013 1:15pm

I went to church this morning. It felt so good to just be there. I have been obedient to my husband and stayed in so much and done so very little in the way of getting out. But I am ready to reclaim my life. Only problem is, I got so tired I just wanted my bed by the time service was over. That's okay, I will continue to do what I can and build my strength back up. I will make it. This chemo is supposed to be almost over for me and I have to rebuild my life.

People here in town will be happy to see me get out some more. The food ministry has run so slow the past several months.

It is Sunday, think I will keep this short and get a nap in. Love you all. Be blessed

You Can't Out love the Lord
By Ida Helton — Jun 10, 2013 9:27am

We teach our kids to sing, 'Jesus Loves Me'. We tell them He loves you this much as we spread our arms wide. We give them many examples of Jesus' love. But do we show that love to our fellow-man?

If you are teaching your child about Christ's love for us, then you must remember that when your neighbors make you angry, or your family displeases you. It's not just for inside your immediate family. It's for all the people in your life. It should matter when you know another person is hungry, thirsty or cold. It should matter when others hurt or need prayer. You must teach your child what really matters.

1 Corinthians 13:4-6 NKJV says, "Love suffers long and is kind; love does not envy; love does not parade itself, is not puffed up; does not behave rudely, does not seek its own, is not provoked, thinks no evil; does not rejoice in iniquity, but rejoices in the truth; bears all things, believes all things, hopes all things, endures all things."

We must teach our children to love one another without boasting about it and being all up and proud because we did it. It's a delicate balance, but so necessary.

My parents taught us love, taught us to love others above ourselves, and taught us to share with others even when we didn't have much for ourselves. But my daddy also taught us to watch and listen, we should know the difference between a person truly needing help with food and maybe gas money, and someone who just uses others for all they can get.

Anyway, I am feeling somewhat better this morning, the Fibromyalgia is beginning to relax, my abdomen still hurts but the doctor is working on the root cause, since it doesn't seem to be the Lymphoma. All things considered it's a great day to be here.

I love you all, be blessed and have a great day.

Jeremiah 33:3
By Ida Helton — Jun 12, 2013 10:21am

People call me, or contact me online, or come to the house. I have the food bank for hungry folks, and I take prayer requests to pass on to others. I am always happy to do it. But, the food bank runs on donations of food and money, and the prayer request is dependent upon who I can contact at that hour. It is always easy to volunteer, not always so easy to find everyone. But I do all I can to make sure we cover the need.

My parents phone number is the same as it was 20 years ago. I can call them and talk to them at any time. Whether they can help me with any problem is limited to what they have at that point in time, and whether I can reach them by phone. If they are outside working in the garden, I may not reach them for hours. Sometimes they have the audacity to go off and be out of town without us being able to contact them (after all, I always had to tell them where I was). I love them, and I call them when I need them, and I stay in touch, but they don't always have an answer to my need.

Our pastor is always reachable by telephone, but he doesn't have all the answers either. Even my best friends do not have the answers. I can talk until I am blue in the face and no one will have the answers.

But, read this verse, "Call to Me (God), and I will answer you, and show you great and mighty things, which you do not know" (Jeremiah 33:3) KJV.

God's phone number is Jeremiah 33:3. Call Me, don't be afraid you can call me, maybe it's late but just call me. Call me and I'll be around. He always answers. He always listens. He is always there, waiting to show us many things which may astound us.

I have not ceased to call on Him during the past several months, because I need something that no man or woman can give me, complete healing. Now, as I am nearing the end of the chemo schedule, we find this did not take care of the pain in my abdomen which has been there for so long. Last week I had an EGD (upper GI) done, and they found nothing. Now they are scheduling a colonoscopy, because they are not happy with what is going on inside me. Awesome Joe and I are disappointed because this has flared up badly again, and we thought the chemo would take care of it. But to deal with the pain I must go to bed and stay there. So, if you don't hear from me it's because I am staying in bed and trying to get past this again, (and all the time calling on God for my healing).

I love you all, and I covet your prayers at this time, because we must find the source of the pain, or God must heal me. That's all there is to that.

Joy
By Ida Helton — Jun 13, 2013 12:05pm

I am creating something new in you; a bubbling Spirit of Joy that spills over into other people's lives. Do not mistake this joy for your own or try to take credit for it in any way. Instead, watch in delight as my Spirit flows through you to bless others. Let yourself become a reservoir of the Spirit's fruit.

Isaiah 43:19 BSB, "Behold, I am about to do something new; even now it is coming. Do you not see it? Indeed, I will make a way in the wilderness and streams in the desert."

I had to share this because so many have asked me how I can remain so positive and upbeat with the Lymphoma and all that is going on. Well, here it is. Thank you, Bro. Dan Tarno, for sharing this today on your Facebook page. I truly believe my strength comes from Him, and that He is my source for ALL things. I rely on Him for ALL, not just a portion.

The first thing Awesome Joe and I did was pray and ask God's leading in this, and then I got our pastor Jerry Truett on the phone and we prayed. I have had prayers from everywhere in the world. I am continuing to press forward with the Spirit of Joy which He (Jesus Christ) has given me, and I will cling to it continually pressing forward. My life is in HIS hands.

In the movie Facing the Giants the song is used "O what I would do to have... " I am a winner. The Voice of Truth tells me a different story from what the doctors and the naysayers say. I have a testimony to tell.

I can't wait to have enough energy and strength to stand in front of my church, and others, and to share what God has done for me the past 6 months. It is truly awesome. He must really love me to have stayed with me throughout all of this.

My nephew, Clevern McBride, and his wife Kayce are expecting another child somewhere around December. It's too early for the doctors to say boy or girl yet, but I said it's a girl. I can't wait to hold her and to see if God has told her about me before she came to her parents. I want to hold her and look at her face and tell her I love her.

I am excited about life and all that is ahead of me. This little bit of pain is negligible when compared to what is ahead.

I love you all.

Enjoy today, One day at a time
By Ida Helton — Jun 14, 2013 8:10am

We are never promised tomorrow. As a matter of fact, anything could happen at any time. When God calls your name, you are leaving here. I read of a 9-year-old girl who was killed in a car accident. So sad and my heart breaks for her family and friends. You will hear many people say she was taken too early. It feels that way. But the truth is, God had her life planned from the beginning. She was only on loan from Heaven.

I am on loan. I hope and pray that I bless others while I am here, but I am only here on loan, and I must work to fulfill my life's meaning and work while I am here. My days were numbered from the beginning. Your days are numbered, and God knows when He will call you home.

The Bible says that no man knows the hour or the day. It also says Jesus himself is waiting for the Father to say, "Son, go get my children." Jesus does not know what the day or hour is. Only God knows.

I am trusting God for a complete healing in Jesus Name, but I am ready for whatever He has planned for me.

The past several weeks have been rough, but I am making it and by the Grace of God I am still standing. Almost finished with the chemo and then my body will need to heal itself from what the chemo has done, but I am fine otherwise. Thank God for His eternal plans for me and my life.

I love you all.

Father's Day
By Ida Helton — Jun 16, 2013 3:35pm

I first apologize, my computer has not been cooperating with me and so I have not been on line in a few days. My health is okay, just internet problems, she said laughing out loud.

I am so excited about this day. I have had 3 wonderful dads: my daddy who passed in 1986, my papa who passed in 2009, and now Pop. Don Evans married my mom in 1987, and it wasn't the best for some of them, but I took him to be my Papa, and when he died my heart broke. Each of them has made some kind of provision for my Mom and she is taken care of now until her time comes to go home. My Daddy and she were married 36 years, Mom lives on his Social Security. She was married to Papa 21 years, and they had savings and his health insurance supplement takes care of her. She and Leon are very happy together and he takes really good care of her at all times. He walks beside her, helps her on steps, he even clips and polishes her toenails. I love how he loves her.

Each of the three men has helped my mom to pray for us, to love us, to provide for us, and to be there for us when we needed her. They treat us like family. It helps me much to know that Mom is taken care of and that Leon is there for her.

My Awesome Joe is the same way. He has been my strong-arm and my buckler throughout all of this. He has prayed with me, held me, made sure I have the help I need throughout all of this. He has been there for me. He is the only one I have told my fears and prayers to, and he has been the one to kick me back into shape when I got down. My constant prayer is that his children are supporting him while he supports me. I know they love their dad, but I am never sure about how they are reacting to this situation especially since their mother died in early 2003 and they miss her. He is the father I would have wanted my children to have. He loves them and prays for them at all times, and we always discuss how he feels about things.

God had a plan when he made daddies. As Pastor Jerry Truett said this morning, we should be parents that our children can talk to, but moms should let the dads be dad and dad should handle their children at some time. Children should always know they can talk to their dads.

Dad should be husband to mom and father to the children. That was God's plan, and when we start to live that way again in the family then we may get back to living as free Americans.

Happy Father's Day.

I love you all.

Rain on the Way
By Ida Helton — Jun 17, 2013 9:05am

It's beginning to rain, Hear the voice of My Savior, He's promised to pour His Spirit out on your sons and your daughters. If you're thirsty and dry look up to the sky, it's beginning to rain.

Spiritual rain is always necessary to keep our souls from becoming dry and thirsty. We have to nourish it daily to keep ourselves going and to keep our faith built up. If you need healing, as I do, then you must keep the faith up. If you pray for others, as I do, your faith must be strong when you start for you to make a difference. One thing I love about our pastor, Jerry Truett, and my husband, is that their prayers get answered.

"The effectual fervent prayer of a righteous man availeth much" (James 5:16 KJV).

One of my friends from childhood posted on Facebook last night that his wife, Mary is in hospital again. Her heart is giving up on her. They are people of faith, and we believe in healing, but this time we have to leave her in God's hands and ask for a miracle. She needs an instant miracle. She is in a medically induced coma and they are testing for brain function. She needs God's instant touch.

Me, I asked God to manifest this healing over a period of months, because I had plenty of time for it, and I didn't see the instant healing. I pray for Mary, but I she is in God's hands.

Our land is about to get physical rain. The sky has become very dark and we are using lights inside to see. They said it is raining in Terrell so hard people are pulling over because they cannot see to drive. I guess we are going to lose internet connection for a while.

I love you all.

Have a very blessed day, and please pray for Mary.

Wow, we're almost there
By Ida Helton — Jun 18, 2013 8:24am

I've had this headache now for about 36 hours. It's how my body is reacting to the chemo. Ready for a break from it. otherwise, I am just waiting for the next round of chemo, which I do on the 26th, 27th and the SHOT on the 28th. I have taken 4 migraine pills this month, and I hadn't had one of those in so long I thought they were behind me.

But my problems are nominal, and easily overcome. Today I am lifting up Mary Boren, the wife of an old friend. Mary had a heart attack a few days ago and has been in hospital, under really strict care since. She needs a miracle. She needs a miracle now. She only has a few more hours before the doctors make a final decision and come to the family with their news. I am praying for all of them. I haven't met her, but I grew up with her husband's family. They are believers. We were all raised in a Pentecostal background. I believe God can give them the miracle they need, but I also know He wrote Mary's life story before she was born and if it is her time to go, then the family will accept that. They know they will see her again. I just pray they don't have to let her go right at this time. It is so hard. Apparently the two grandsons tried to keep her alive while the EMT's came to get her. She was without oxygen for 20 minutes, they said.

I really want the family, the entire family, to be ready, and to not feel they could have done something differently. Please help me to pray for them.

It makes my troubles seem so small and unimportant. After all, my family accepted going in that the chemo might not work. We all knew it could be God's time for me. But He has been gracious and honored our prayers and I am seeing the proof of the healing with each new CT Scan. I thank God for that. I am so blessed. It means there is more work for me to do here. I pray He will guide my steps and keep me moving forward in the right direction. He has saved me for a reason.

I wish you would sign my guestbook, sometimes I feel so alone in the journey. It really helps me to know how many are reading and watching for my posts. I love you all and I depend on your prayers to complete the good work that God has begun in me.

Meditations of My Heart
By Ida Helton — Jun 19, 2013 11:47am

May the words of my mouth and the meditations of my heart be pleasing to you, Oh Lord, My Rock and My Redeemer.

I have tried throughout this ordeal with the Lymphoma and all. I have made sure not to get online when I am feeling down, because I don't want to bring somebody else down, I want to be an inspiration. As the 26th approaches and it comes time for Chemo round 6, my prayers and meditations are turning more and more to seeing positive results in the CT Scan I am sure they will do afterward.

Before this diagnosis, I was in pain so badly more than 90% of the time. Now, some of that has eased. Some is still there. Because of the chemo, I have 3 or 4 bad days to 1 good day. I don't mind, because I know it's for a reason.

So today, my meditations are strictly in praise and thanksgiving. I am so thankful they found this Lymphoma before it could get any worse. I am thankful to know where at least some of the pain was coming from. I am thankful for all the friends and family who have stood with me through this.

Most of all, I am thankful that everyone has been careful to stand in agreement with me and no one has come to me with negative thoughts or words. I said in the beginning this was to hard a battle. Just be positive, that was all I asked. Thank God, you all listened to me and we have made it this far by faith. The next step of this journey is in His hands.

I love you all.

The Lord is My Shepherd
By Ida Helton — Jun 20, 2013 8:39am

Psalm 23 KJV, "The Lord is my Shepherd, I shall not want. He makes me to lie down in green pastures: He leads me beside the still waters. He restores my soul; He leads me in the paths of righteousness For His Name's sake. Yea, though I walk through the valley of the shadow of death, I will fear no evil; For you are with me; Your rod and Your staff they comfort me. You prepare a table before me in the presence of my enemies; You anoint my head with oil; My cup runs over. Surely goodness and mercy shall follow me all the days of my life; and I will dwell in the house of the Lord forever".

He is my Shepherd, I am inn need of nothing. He feeds me, He calms my storms, He gives me peace, He keeps me in His righteousness so that He may be glorified.

But then it says, I can walk through the valley of the shadow of death and fear no evil, for God is with me at all times. He comforts me with a rod and a staff. (Just like a shepherd calms his lambs).

I love this passage of Scripture so much, He is my Shepherd, and He is always with me. I will dwell with Him forever.

I have faced all of this with the comfort that no man could have given me because of Him. Because of Him, because of my knowledge of Him through Scripture and Word, I can jump through a troop and leap over a wall. What could a little bit of cancer possibly do to me? And, after all, either way, I win.

I only asked that I might see my child and grandchildren and their families serving HIM, and I believe we are about halfway there. I will take it any way it comes.

I love you all.

I abide in His secret place
By Ida Helton — Jun 21, 2013 11:57am

Psalm 91:1 NKJV, "He who dwells in the secret place of the Most High, shall abide in the shadow of the Almighty"...

He is my fortress and my stronghold. He gave me Awesome Joe to lean on and to hold my hand, and then He said abide in me, I will go with you through the storm.

I have stayed in His shadow through this. I am not willing to get out of that place. Joe and I have talked, but only God has been privy to my most private thoughts and prayers in this.

Thank you all for supporting me with prayer, love and friendship, I couldn't do this without you. I think of you as holding my elbows up, much as Aaron helped to hold Moses up during a battle.

I love you all.

The Lord will watch over me...
By Ida Helton — Jun 22, 2013 3:42pm

The Lord will keep you from all harm - He will watch over your life

"The Lord will watch over your coming and going both now and forevermore."

Psalm 121: 7-8 NKJV

I trust Him to watch over me at all times. He put His angels all around me to keep me from harm and so that no evil would befall me. I need to have a few more tests run, and that is okay, anything that helps me to deal with this pain in my abdomen. I just know that my Father is watching over me now as He always has, and I am in His hands, both now and forevermore.

What a wonderful thought, to be forever in His care. I trust that care so much more than I trust mankind. Men can fail you, God has never failed me yet. He never will.

Have a great day and be blessed.

Sunday Morning
By Ida Helton — Jun 23, 2013 8:38am

Time to get up and go to church. If you haven't done anything else all week you need to get up and get yourself in gear. Church is today, and it's important because next week I just can't go as I will be straight out of chemo.

So today, I got up and took a bath and I am getting myself ready to go pick up Hannah and the two of us will go to church. Hannah is a 15-year-old teenager who I love as if she were my own. She has been going to church with me for two years. She really loves the Lord and really prays for her friends and family to come along. She is a good example of what kids are supposed to be. She is a star in the band percussion group, getting ready to go to college and smart. She wants to be a Pediatric Oncologist, so my journey is helping her to learn.

Anyway, it's a beautiful day, the sun is really shining bright and it is time to get ready for church.

This pain in my side is getting worse, not better, and I can't wait to go to the next step to find out what it is. Joyce at Walmart told me to ask my oncologist about a PET Scan instead of the colonoscopy, she said it is much less invasive and will give them a better picture without all that putting me to sleep and then additional testing if the first one doesn't work. I think I will do so on Wednesday when I go in. He has been pretty good to listen to me so far, but I haven't asked for anything.

I just want the pain to resolve itself and I want to know where it comes from. NOW. This has been an ongoing thing for several years and I just need a break. Laugh out loud. I guess I will get one when I lay down for my final rest but that's a long time away. when they diagnosed all these tumors, Joe and I immediately decided that must have been the problem, but pain is still there and now it is getting stronger all the time.

Anyway. I love you all and will talk to you again soon. God bless you.

I am not ashamed
By Ida Helton — Jun 24, 2013 9:19am

I am not ashamed (of the Gospel) because I know whom I have believed...

Don't ask if you don't want to know. I am able to walk and talk and laugh and be positive because I know who holds all my tomorrows and I know who holds my hands today. I am saved by the Grace of God and I am ready to admit it and to shout it to anyone who wants to know. Don't tell me how good your life is without my Jesus in it, because I know how bad your future is.

It's funny, one of the things on Facebook was to share when and where we got saved and I remember it vividly. I was 8 years old and we were at First Assembly of God Church in Wilmer, Texas. I remember we were in revival. I went to the altar and when I finally came back I told my parents I was going to be a missionary. Now, at 60+, I have the food ministry and the soup ministry was pretty strong. We serve people and we are free to tell them about the Lord. I am doing Missionary work right here in Myrtle Springs. When I lived in Memphis, I talked to people daily about my faith and what God has done for me. I was doing missionary work there. It seems I have always done some kind of missionary work, although most of us think of missionary work as overseas. Not me, I work right here at home. I bloom where I am planted and let God do the rest.

This Lymphoma has given me a big chance to talk to people I would not normally see. The patients and nurses at the Oncology Clinic are wonderful, and I love to share with them how God has helped me through this. They tell me their own stories. I am building quite a memory of work to help others.

My childhood friend, Jerry Boren, lost his wife last week to cardiac problems, and complications. I saw in his response the work of a minister. He never posted anything negative or down. In fact, he is still blessing me this morning with his words. This is what a true believer should be able to do.

"IN EVERYTHING GIVE THANKS, FOR THIS IS THE WILL OF GOD IN CHRIST JESUS" (1 Thessalonians 5:18 NKJV). Give thanks, for all you know, someone may be watching and need to see your response to see if you are for real.

I start Chemo again on Wednesday.

I love you all.

CHEMO IS FINISHED
By Ida Helton — Jun 26, 2013 5:41pm

Tomorrow is my last day of CHEMO.... I still have to do Colonoscopy, Doctor is ordering a PET Scan which I will have to take, follow up with doctor in 4 weeks, then maintenance is about 90 minutes every 8 weeks. The maintenance is a something called Rituxan, an antibody. You still take it like Chemo, but it is not chemo. I may get to ring the bell tomorrow. If so, you will see a picture on Face book.

I am so totally blessed. Only by God's grace am I here. I am tee totally wallowing like a pig in the grace of Almighty God.

I am also very tired, Today was my long day, so I have been on the move since 5:30. Chemo is so hard on the body. Thank God I am free, Free, FREE. Thank you, Lord.

A Very Blessed Day
By Ida Helton — Jun 27, 2013 9:49am

God is good, He hath done me well, Oh, my soul, rise up and praise the Lord.

We used to sing that little line in church all the time. I loved it then and today it means so much more to me. He is good. He hath done me well. I have come through the hardest part of this journey. Yesterday the doctor looked at me and said, "If I didn't know it, and know your chart, I would not believe you have been in Chemo for 6 months. You don't look like it."

That's just God doing what He does. He makes me look good.

Yesterday and today are round 6 of the chemo and today is my last. Thank you, Lord. That stuff has done some awful things to my body, but I have kept up and tried to keep going.

I still have two years of maintenance, going back every 2 months for the Rituxan and the checkups and blood work, and all that. But NO More CHEMO for now. My 6 months are up, and it is time to start the recovery. AMEN.

He said it will not be an immediate up, might take several months yet, but at least it will come. I should have the PET Scan one day in July and then we will know for sure if everything is gone or if we have more work to do. For now, I am just praising God for His blessings to me.

Won't you all join me? I feel a major weight lifted off of me now, and even Awesome Joe is excited. He wants his wife back, I think. I am ready.

I love you all. Have a VERY BLESSED DAY.

Truly Blessed
By Ida Helton — Jun 28, 2013 6:22pm

I am blessed. I am so blessed. I am so truly blessed. I am so truly, truly blessed. I am so truly, Truly BLESSED.

When I started on this journey, I knew in my heart that it would take faith, and prayer and a lot of support from everybody. I knew to get through to the next big step.

I have an appointment for the PET Scan on Wednesday morning, and then the colonoscopy doctor on the 17th. The Oncologist wants that done before we go any further. Then I follow up with him on the 24th of July. After that the maintenance is every 2 months, an infusion of Rituxan which will take about 2 hours and checking with doctors and labs. That will last 2 years.

I just want the recovery to get started now. I feel an urge to get up and get busy. This journal will turn in to a book, and I will tell people how wonderful it is to wallow in the Amazing Grace of God. I have spent six months bellying up to that bar, drinking from the swill that falls through the cracks in the trough, and just basically wallowing in the slop. Amazing Grace, I have been living in it and cannot get out of it.

I am ready to get out and share with everyone. But the doctor cautions me, and my friends and nurses tell me, I have to be careful here. I have to recover my strength. I want to do all of this right. Maybe I can just work on the book here at home, and then start moving when I get there. I just want to be careful.

I love you all. I am recovering now from the SHOT. I will probably be quiet for a few days.

Rough Day today
By Ida Helton — Jun 29, 2013 7:49pm

It's been a really rough day today. I have stayed in bed and just relaxed. Awesome Joe is here. He has made sure I got waited on and taken care of. My son, Dewayne is still here, so he and his boys have helped me too. That SHOT is a killer for me. I deal with pain from the top of my head to the bottom of my feet. There is nausea and chills and everything else you can imagine.

I am so ready for this to go away, but I probably have about 3 to 4 more days, and then I have the PET Scan scheduled for Wednesday. In preparation for that, I have to drop off carbohydrates, sugars and all caffeine. Personally, I do the Low Carb diet most of the time, so they could have the carbs and the sugars. But what do you mean NO CAFFEINE? They had better come armed with a straight jacket. Seriously, can't imagine anything worse than doing without both for several days.

Anyway, this is the first time my Awesome Joe has been here immediately following the chemo sessions. They are pretty rough on me, and it takes me several days to get back on my feet.

Can't wait to get the results of the PET Scan and know that everything is completely gone.

There is also a Colonoscopy coming later this month. I am Not Looking forward to that.

God has been good to me; the chemo sessions are over. Now the work really begins.

Still resting
By Ida Helton — Jun 30, 2013 5:05pm

My Awesome Joe asked me this morning how long this would last. I told him it would be 3 to 4 days. He really frowned and grunted. He hates to see me in this kind of pain. That SHOT forces the bone marrow to produce white blood cells and it hurts. Only relief I have gotten this time is to completely knock myself out with pain pills and muscle relaxers, and I have taken medication for migraine twice. So glad this was that last SHOT I have to take.

I must try to get out of bed tomorrow, if only for a little while.

I love you all.... Thank you for your prayers.

I am up... but only for a short
By Ida Helton — Jul 1, 2013 8:05am

I got up with Awesome Joe, he had to go into Dallas to deliver the last of his freight. I can only stay up a short while, and then the spasms start, and I can't move and, right now, there is no one here to help me.

I sat at the table to eat grilled burgers and hot dogs with them last night and Corey had to pull me out of the chair and almost carried me to bed. It is really bad. And this makes the Fibromyalgia go absolutely crazy. I am trying to get back on my feet, but it will be a process this time.

- My wonderful hubby thinks I should just stay in bed for a few days and let it work its way through my body, and I wish it would work that way. I am afraid if I stay down, I will be down and can't get back up. I love him, and he has really had to watch me suffer these past few days.

- I told him he just chose the wrong week to stay home. I have been trying to tell him how bad it was over the phone, and then I would say I have to go, because I am in too much pain to talk. Not this time, he is seeing it all right up close and personal.
- I feel so bad for him. He watches me try to get around the house with the cane (and I really do look like an old lady). It's really funny to see in the mirror.

My one redeeming thought here is that God is still on His throne, and all is right with His world. Everything is working according to His plan for my good, and I must be patient and walk through this journey without moaning and groaning. I am really trying to do that.

I can't keep taking migraine medicine and pain pills, I have to get my body to moving. I suggested to him that I should run a marathon while he is gone this morning. He laughed and said he would pick me up before I got to the end of the driveway. We are really trying to keep our humor here.

My biggest problem is that the SHOT and the Fibromyalgia don't seem to want to be in my body at the same time. But they don't have a choice. It's my body and I told it to behave.

My family is making some big plans for Christmas this year. On the 21st of December, we will meet at the old school building in Myrtle Springs, and my brothers and sisters will all be there. Martha is the only one we have a question about, and I think she will work it out with her boss in Michigan. It is time for all to be together again. We need to pay attention to our mom's health, and my journey here has really scared a few people. Come on December. This is Martha and her very own Awesome Joe.

I love you all. Hope someone is reading this. Hope and pray some of it blesses you. I know it has helped me to be able to keep writing my journal. Thanks.

I AM UP, THANKS BE TO GOD
By Ida Helton — Jul 2, 2013 11:55am

Well, I am finally up. I think I will take another day very easily. I can stand up without using my cane or being pulled, I can walk inside without the cane again. I actually got up at 8 this morning and went outside and spent about 15 minutes on my roses. They need a few hours, but I felt it wise to stop when I did.

I went to bed around 9 last night, taking yet another muscle relaxer and pain pill on the way. I woke up around 4 and was back asleep by 4:30 without extra medication. Then I woke up around 8 to April barking and having a fit, seems Daddy got way to close to her Hopping Hips treat that she takes every morning. He had to give it to her, of course, and then I said, "what time is it?"

I was so shocked when he told me I had slept until 8, but my body is really tired and weary after that last round of chemo and the SHOT. I can laugh now, but it wasn't pleasant there for a few days.

But God, in His mercy, has let me see the worst of it, and now I will be feeling better.

I am doing the PREP WORK for the PET Scan now. That means today I can't have any carbohydrates, no sugars, and no caffeine. They really believe in cruel and unusual punishment. But the PET is scheduled for 11:45 and then I can have some caffeine.

Now for good news. Awesome Joe and I are having our 10th anniversary on Friday the 5th. We have Big Plans. We are getting our portrait made in Tyler. I am so excited. I can't tell you that it's been an easy 10 years. We have had our storms, mostly from outside sources trying to pull us apart, but because we love each other and feel this is where God wants us, we have made it. These are the best years of my life. We have learned to work together to overcome adversity and to see life through each other's eyes.

I have wanted a professional portrait for a long time, and he always said no. I believe the battle of the past 6 months has shown him how very fragile our situation really is, and he just said yes. (I have our portrait clothes picked out and ready to go, my little black dress, and his black western shirt with bright white piping. We are going to look so good, every person in the world is going to be jealous.

I read 1Peter 5:7 NKJV, this morning. "CASTING ALL YOUR CARES UPON HIM FOR HE CARES FOR YOU". In the beginning of this journey, my first step was to give everything to Him and to say, "this is my life, and I want your will in it." I haven't stopped feeling that way. My life has been spared for a little while, or for many years to come. It is up to me to use these days and years to do His will, and to lead people home to His loving arms. I can't wait to get out there and get busy, but the hardest part is the recuperation. Those days when you look fine and everybody thinks you are okay, but you don't feel like doing anything, because your body is recovering from the trauma of the past several months. They told me this could take a few months to a year. My instructions are to stop and rest and don't let myself go too far, and I am really going to try, because I don't want any relapse or new problems.

I love you all.

PET Scan is done
By Ida Helton — Jul 4, 2013 9:03am

I can only pray about the results. The test is done. Thank God, He has brought me this far and He will see me through.

I still have to get through a few more tests, because the pain in my side is not gone away, and then we shall know what is going on inside me now that the chemo is done.

MAINTENANCE HERE I COME.

Our 10th Anniversary
By Ida Helton — Jul 5, 2013 1:18pm

Yes, we did. We made it with God's grace and mercy, we made 10 years. Our families seem to have been our biggest trials, why can't they just let grownups be grownups and be happy? But all in all, it's been the best 10 years of my life.

God saw fit to put us together, knowing I would need a strong man to lead me or I wouldn't follow. He knew our faith was strong enough to keep our eyes on Him when all else was going crazy around us. He knows exactly how much stress we can take before we have to tell them all to butt out.

And He knew that Joe, My Awesome Joe, would be able to stand up to my trials and hold my hand as I face the Fibromyalgia and the Lymphoma and all the other things that have come at us. But, we are still here.

My life is so blessed. Still waiting for results of the PET Scan, they did tell me it would probably be Monday. This is the first day I have actually been able to walk 2 feet without the cane to help me. I actually feel pretty good.

We are going to Tyler to have portraits made. Lisa Miller was so sweet to come and trim my hair and style it for me and to do my makeup this morning. I am professionally done up for this picture and it better look good. Even Awesome Joe got a haircut. We are so excited, to be able to celebrate 10 years like this, and together.

I am feeling better and will talk to all of you tomorrow. Love you.

Quiet Day Today
By Ida Helton — Jul 6, 2013 3:13pm

Still trying to catch my next wind. Going with Joe yesterday was fun, but it wore me out. I promised I would be quiet for the weekend. That means I am staying down and resting. He didn't need my promise, I am too tired to move

FEELING BETTER!
By Ida Helton — Jul 10, 2013 9:58am

Yeah, Finally I can see the light of day. Wow, two full weeks to even start to see the recovery from that last session, and it really did knock me for loops. I have stayed home except for going with Awesome Joe on our anniversary to have portraits made. He made it easy to do this, because he does all the driving and I get to rest. And of course, there was the day for the PET Scan, but again, he did the driving.

Awesome Joe is in California now though, and he won't be staying home for at least another month. That means my friend Marie will drive me. It's just not the same, but she tries.

Now. For my report. The PET Scan results should be in, but the doctor has not called me, so I am not sure what they found. I have a call in to the doctor and should know something later today.

God has been good throughout this. He is ever-faithful. He has taken care of me, and other than the fatigue and now this pain in my abdomen, there haven't been a lot of negatives through this time. The doctor is determined, as am I, to find the source of the pain. It just won't stop. It varies in degree from just a nagging pain, to an absolutely nauseating pain that can't be stopped.

If it weren't for knowing that God is on my side, there would have been times to quit, times to withdraw from life, but with Him on my side I have come through with faith ever stronger that it was in the beginning and I feel so blessed to have survived this traumatic time in our lives. I am blessed.

PET SCAN RESULTS
By Ida Helton — Jul 10, 2013 3:23pm

Praise God. Praise God. Praise God. I am Cancer free. The PET Scan shows there is no cancer left anywhere in my body. I have finished Chemo, but still have to do the maintenance, and they are still looking for the reason for the pain in my abdomen, but it is not cancer. The cancer and tumors are completely GONE. God is good, all the time.

JEREMIAH 32:17
By Ida Helton — Jul 11, 2013 10:03am

"Ah, Sovereign Lord, You have made the heavens and the earth by your great power and outstretched arm. NOTHING IS TOO HARD FOR YOU" (Jeremiah 32:17). I give all praise, honor and glory to God. The Lymphoma has been removed from my body. I am now CANCER FREE. God has done a great work for me, and in me.

I thank you all for your prayers and your support. I am now in recovery and will have 2 years of maintenance, but no cancer cells in my body. That is a miracle. Thank you, Lord for your mercies to me.

I love you all.

It's another Doctor Day
By Ida Helton — Jul 17, 2013 11:00am

Today I go to Gastroenterologist. Corey and Sandra will be taking me. They are supposed to be scheduling the Colonoscopy, trying to figure out why I still have so much pain in my abdomen. I had it in spells before, everyone thought the Chemo would take care of it, but it did not. Now they have to determine what it is.

I know that God is in control here, and it can be easily handled. It hasn't shown on any CT Scan or the PET Scan a few weeks ago. They say it has to be something internal and this is where they start. The only thing I am absolutely certain of is that there is no CANCER in my body. The PET Scan would have shown it and it did not.

I thank God for my healing. He must not have fulfilled His purpose for me yet. Still much work to do here.

Much Better Today
By Ida Helton — Jul 19, 2013 10:31am

As the chemo works its way through my body, I am ready to return to a semblance of life. I had done too much in the previous few days and ended up having to take yesterday completely off. I was completely worn out. But, I thank the Lord I am much better today. Thank you for your continued prayers.

REMISSION
By Ida Helton — Jul 24, 2013 3:47pm

Doctor says I am in REMISSION.

He said this type of Lymphoma can come back at any time or it may never come back. I am no scientist, but I could probably have said that, what I actually said is, "You just have to trust God, because He is the reason it's gone."

I thank you all for your much-needed prayers and support.

Getting Answers
By Ida Helton — Jul 25, 2013 5:09pm

Gastroenterologist says the problem in my abdomen starts with a fatty liver. She made no recommendations, because they are still running tests, so I looked it up. I am going back on the low carbohydrate diet and taking a round of probiotics from the health food store. Hopefully this will help the pain really quickly, because I am ready for a break from it.

From what I read about it, it can range in severity from minor to major liver disease. I personally think the chemo has set it off, because it started after the second treatment and hasn't stopped since. The pain is always there, and sometimes it is accompanied by nausea and a lot of fatigue and weakness. What we have to wait for is to see how much of this resolves itself with my recovery period.

The GOOD NEWS is that I start maintenance on August 8, and after the first treatment they will remove the PICC line. (FOR ALL OF YOU WHO DON'T KNOW THAT MEANS I CAN TAKE A LONG HOT SHOWER IN A FEW WEEKS.) I am not complaining but I miss my showers and running hot water all over me. Yeah... Shower. Then, Awesome Joe says as soon as this hose is out of my arm, he wants me to travel with him for a week or so. Sounds like a real winner to me.

One Day at a Time
By Ida Helton — Jul 29, 2013 8:04am

I plan to live my life One Day at a Time from hence forth. I can't go back and redo anything. I can't do away with months of Chemo or anything else. But from this day forward I can make sure I share God's grace and mercy to me every day. I can't forget all that He has done for me. He has healed my body and made me whole again. I must shout it from the mountain tops.

I am cancer free because of Him and His grace. Because Jesus took those stripes and went to Calvary. I am free of cancer. Because of His mercy I am alive to tell the story.

I can't wait for the recovery to be complete so that I can shout it from the mountain tops.

Testing tomorrow...
By Ida Helton — Aug 6, 2013 7:58am

Well, the big day is almost here. Tomorrow is my day to go for the Colonoscopy. For those of you who have had one, you know that means today and yesterday are 'body prep' days. Basically, yesterday was liquid (including ice cream) anything that is liquid in its natural state they said. Today is clear liquids. That means jello and broth. Not too big on the broth but will do some for strength.

My poor Awesome Joe doesn't know whether to just go out somewhere to eat or to ask someone to come cook for just him. He's just not used to me not being in the kitchen, but right now that is intolerable for me.

I sincerely hope that when they talk to us post-testing tomorrow they have some definitive answers, because this pain in my side is often unbearable. I don't think it has stopped completely in over 5 months. We all thought it would go away as the chemo progressed, but it has not.

I am praying for an answer that I can hand to my Father and say why would you take the Lymphoma and leave this. We know it is not cancer because there was no uptake of the die anywhere in my body. That means no cancer anywhere. Praise God for that.

On Thursday I start the maintenance and after the infusion of Rituxan they are supposed to remove the PICC line from my arm. Awesome Joe calls this my hose. Once that is gone, I go back every two months for an infusion of the Rituxan, but they do it by IV. I will be free to go.

God is so good to me and He has taught me great and mighty things through this journey. I can't wait to get to the important stuff, writing it all down.

It's the liver...
By Ida Helton — Aug 10, 2013 11:40am

I am praying and asking prayers again. Apparently, the chemo and other medicines that I take, and the way I eat (on steroids) have caused my liver to act up, which is now causing my spleen to be slightly enlarged. They say this condition is usually not accompanied by pain, but then they don't know me.

Truth is, no one has so far even suggested how to work on the problem, and my next appointment with the GI doctor is in October, while my next appointment with the Oncologist is in September.

I have prayed, and I have sought the Lord in this matter, and I have decided to try to flush my liver with mostly vegetarian diet for a few months, with Milk Thistle from health food store, and with apple juice and bananas. I feel that I must let the liver rest from all the other stuff and from processing hard meat and foods. Hopefully this will get things moving along properly again.

There is good news, THE PICC LINE IS GONE. I go back for an infusion of Rituxan every other month and they took the PICC out because of too much risk for infection. In other news, my ANC (immunology numbers) have dropped because of the purging and cleanse for the procedure done earlier this week, so I am basically back at home resting for at least 2 more weeks. YUK. But I have to be careful not to get an infection because I have very little to fight it with.

I won't be going to church tomorrow, or to do my shopping today. But that is okay because Jesus knows where I am, and He talks to me here.

I love you all.

Maintenance has started...
By Ida Helton — Aug 14, 2013 8:32am

It's hit me almost as hard as the chemo did every month. That juice they ran into me is hard on the body, and my body made sure I knew it. LOL. I have been just plain down the past few days.

Of course, they told me my immunity was way down again and that I must protect myself from any infection. Then they ran the infusion of Rituxan and I felt fine for a little while, but the longer it is in my body, the more I feel like mud.

My friend told me I must have thought the hard part was over and I was "free to go". Well, I guess that was right. I knew there was a healing time coming, and that I would need to recover, but I never thought I would feel like this after the maintenance.

Anyway, God has been good to me and my abdominal pain is now beginning to ease itself up. I am sure the Chemo set off an existing problem and now the Chemo is over the problem may work itself out. I hope so. That was a kicker every time. I am trying to do kind of a flush of the liver and make sure all the stuff clears out and I pray the wisdom of God over the situation because the doctors don't seem to have a clue.

Please, keep me in your prayers. I am healing now, but it may take a while.

Recovery is going slow...
By Ida Helton — Aug 17, 2013 11:31am

I thank God that I am in remission. I thank God that everything went so well throughout the treatment. Other than the fatigue I was basically all right. Now, will someone please tell my body we don't have to do all that anymore.

I went with Awesome Joe on Thursday to Greenville, we had his daughter and two grandsons with us. There was a point where I just doubled up and had to return to the vehicle and sit there. I was down all day yesterday and today is not looking any better. I am simply worn out. I knew my immunity was down, and I had to be careful, I just didn't realize what those few hours would do to my body.

I will be staying home for at least several more days. There is no way I am pushing past this point and making myself really sick.

Thank you all for your continued prayers.

Immunity and Recovery
By Ida Helton — Sep 10, 2013 10:15am

Well, it's been 2 1/2 months since I had the last chemo, and I am feeling better. At my follow-up on Friday, the Oncologist told me my immunity is still way down. Evidently being CANCER FREE does not solve that issue very quickly. They told me to make sure I get a flu shot, and if anyone gets the mist I have to stay away from them for 30 days.

All my grandkids and family are getting shot during this week. So, I trekked off to Walmart yesterday only to discover they haven't started there yet. Maybe today I can get into CVS and get it there. Not sure. But my parents got theirs really fast, then Mom called and said, "are you coming over right now?" She has such a beautiful sense of humor. I had to admit I am worn out and waiting for another burst of energy.

The liver has finally begun to settle down (they keep telling me the liver does not hurt) and I am feeling much stronger. Please continue to pray for that area, and for my recovering strength.

I really think about a lot of things while I am sitting at home doing much of nothing. I want you all to know that God has richly blessed me with my health and my life and my family. In the words of a song, GOD TAKES GOOD CARE OF ME.

Over the past several months I have missed a lot of things, my sister got married and I was too sick to travel the 100 miles to be there for her. I have stayed home from church, and let others do all my shopping and running. I am so thankful that I can finally do for myself again, and I know to stop when I get tired. (I've learned the hard way.). If I don't stop when I start getting tired, I end up down for several days. But if I stop at that point and rest, then I have the time to recover and go again.

The kids are back in school, the adults are taking care of themselves and Awesome Joe is working his plan. He has hired a man who just wants to take it easy, wants to drive every other week. That means Joe gets to stay home every other week and rest. I am enjoying getting to know him again, because there has been a lot of alone time for both of us this past 8 months. I thank God for my Awesome Joe, and we love each other, but he was driving the truck and I was here, resting or taking chemo. Many days I didn't have the strength to even talk to him on the phone. Now I am getting to cuddle up to him at night and go to sleep in his arms. That is wonderful news to me, I have missed him so much.

I want to thank you all for your continued prayer and support. Recovery is, in some ways, harder than the chemo for me, but I am blessed to be at this stage. I love you all.

Trusting God for Healing
By Ida Helton — Oct 15, 2013 8:49am

I am trusting God, because I am nothing without Him. He has taken the cancer from my body. I am so very blessed.

Now, the maintenance is really getting me. Had the treatment on the 4th of October. Today is the 15th. I am still weak and tired. I have a headache. I can't sleep. Just really need a touch from God.

Also, I am not taking blood pressure medicine right now, and they have to give me steroids with the treatment. I think I will go back to Doctor Dailey and get something for the blood pressure. My temper is so very unreasonably short, my family has decided to stay away from me. Even Awesome Joe is avoiding me now.

I really need to get some help. I am not an angry person. I hate people who live on a short trigger, but mine is not even reasonable. I get angry at the computer, at the news, at the kids for breathing. It really takes too much from me to try to calm down. I must get a grip on this.

God has been so good to me on every single issue. I must honor Him with my obedience, and this temper thing has to go away. Besides, the sweats are back, and I can't really live in a pool of sweat water. Yep, time to go back to doctor. He will need to add medicines back, but at least my family will love me again.

I trust that each of you is enjoying this beautiful fall weather. I really want so much for my friends and family, and happiness is at the top of the list.

Love you all. Please keep praying.

My healing, My faith
By Ida Helton — Nov 22, 2013 4:43pm

Well it's been quite a journey. I had chest pains in October, which thankfully turned out to be nothing. They scared me with phone calls and tests, but God took care of it before they could run tests. The Heart Catheterization showed no blockages, no plaque buildup, and very strong heart. Doctor said mine is functioning at the top of the margins. He was impressed. They finally said it had to be another reaction to the chemo or Fibromyalgia. I am fine.

I trust that I am a witness to all I meet. I wouldn't want to make it about me, because I am nothing, but with HIM at my side, and inside and with me, I am and can do ALL things. I'm a believer.

My Testimony
By Ida Helton — Jan 5, 2014 3:08pm

What a blessing it is to know that my testimony is touching other's lives. On the 2nd, Wednesday, I went to Texas Oncology. As I was waiting to sign in, another lady came through the door, I didn't know her, but she was with 2 of the ladies from our church. She told me that she was on her 3rd diagnosis of cancer, and that she had gotten very depressed when they told her. She was trying to pull herself up and get happy again. I started sharing my testimony, and she was so excited. One of the ladies with her said, "This is Ida, the one we have been telling you about." That blessed me, to know that my story is encouraging others.

I have known all my life that when we put His Words in our heart and spirit, they will rise up when needed and they will give us all we need. The verse that rose up in me at the first diagnosis meeting was simple, "I know the plans I have for you says the Lord." Jeremiah 29:11. The doctor said you have limited lifetime expectations. I said, "you didn't write my life story." God planned my life before He created the world. You can't change His plans for me.

I hate to hear people say someone died before their time, or that they were too young. God numbered our days before we were born. We must accept that.

I want my life to be a testimony that I believe He planned it, knows my decisions before I make them. But He loves me enough to allow me to do it. Even when He knows my decision is wrong. He lets me be free to do it. When I come back and say I was wrong, He just opens His arms wide and lets me in. I have never heard God say, "I told you so."

I face 2014 with great anticipation and expectation. I know that God is guiding me and calling me. I have a job to do, my story must be told. It is for everyone to be encouraged and uplifted. We need more people testifying of God's greatness and mercy, and less people complaining.

Thank you all for your support.

New doctor today
By Ida Helton — Jan 8, 2014 9:22am

After many years of trusting my doctor to care about my health and my body, I have to go to a new doctor today. I wonder if she will be the right one. When I first met my doctor, I couldn't get up out of a chair. I couldn't walk upright. He found the problem and has treated it all these years. When I would call and need help, I didn't have to wait, I just got right in. Now, I have to trust someone else to care about me like that. Please pray for me. I am very nervous about this. '

He worked it out.
By Ida Helton — Jan 13, 2014 11:17am

My new doctor is good, and I am pleased to announce that she seemed to care about me. She asked me questions about my file and prescribed the medicines I need. I am okay with the change, even though I hate to lose Dr. Dailey. He has taken care of me for a long time.

I was reading this morning about the woman with the issue of blood. This woman was a cast away. She was not ever supposed to come close to her fellow people. If she touched them, she could be stoned to death. But, she didn't let that stop her. She continued to press forward until she got close enough to just touch his garment. She didn't get to touch him, only His garment. He felt the virtue of healing leave Him.

She pressed forward in faith, despite all the odds and all the laws against it. Matthew 9:20-22 tells us the story. When He felt the healing virtue leave Him, He turned to her. His Words, "Be of good cheer, daughter, your faith has made you whole." He healed her because of her faith. He felt her faith drawing on His Spirit. This lesson is important. If you hear a doctor pronounce a life-sentence, if you need financial help, you want to see your family saved, whatever... whatever you need or want. I believe God hears our first prayer, before we even voice it, but sometimes you have to keep pressing forward until He hears your heart.

Sometimes you have to keep working at getting His Spirit to draw to yours. Sometimes you just have to hold on and keep shouting until the rope begins to be pulled up. Don't give in to the fear of cancer or the notice of overdraft from your bank. Don't give up. Just start praising

Him and pressing forward until He can hear your heart, and then You will know His answer.

Rough Weekend equals Rough Day
By Ida Helton — Jan 20, 2014 11:20am

My weekend was rather busy and stressful. I was not able to move much at all yesterday, and today is easier, but I am still really sore.

I thank God, because they got Dustin into a position that we can get him some help for these mood swings, and he is safe. Even though he was care flighted, it was a minor injury that looked really bad at first. My rough weekend came from all the walking at Methodist Hospital in Dallas.

Thank you, Lord for your protection for us.

Feeling Much Better
By Ida Helton — Jan 22, 2014 8:08am

And, it's time. I have bookwork to do prior to the 31st and this is severely messing with my schedule. God is Faithful, and He is the Healer. I have called upon Him in my distress and He has heard my cry and He has healed me.

Today, as we finish the process and get things back to normal, we are ready to go forth, fully armed with the Gospel of Christ.

Thank you for your prayers.

I feel good... Hallelujah
By Ida Helton — Jan 23, 2014 4:17pm

It is time to praise the Lord with all my might. I go Wednesday for a CT Scan and have the next maintenance treatment on the 5th of February. Thank you, Lord for good results and for an easy time with the meds. I love You and I trust you completely. After all, FAITH is:
Fully And Implicitly Trusting Him.

How marvelous
By Ida Helton — Jan 24, 2014 10:32am

How wonderful, how marvelous is my Savior's love for me. That will be forever my song.

What a weekend.
By Ida Helton — Jan 27, 2014 10:07am

Fibromyalgia responds to the weather, to stress, and to any slight infection anywhere in your body. When I was first diagnosed with Lymphoma, people would ask how long before I started feeling normal again. My answer is quite simple. I don't know what normal is.

For the past two weeks the family has been in an uproar, and my body is telling me to quit. I can't. I have a few more weeks to go. We get answers on the 14th.

In the meantime, the weather has been so crazy, and the cold is really getting to me. I am embarrassed to say I had friends here this weekend and couldn't even help with simple chores. She did everything.

I know there is a reason for God to have left this when He took the cancer, but I can't think of one. Anyway, I trust Him, He is my source, and He is my Healer. I give this problem to Him. Thank you for joining me in prayer.

Untitled
By Ida Helton — Jan 27, 2014 10:10am

    Two of our kids (adopted grands) came to see me this weekend. We now have a great-grandson who is 8 months old. Luke is a joy to behold. I am so proud of these two.

Music is my Best Friend
By Ida Helton — Jan 28, 2014 1:41pm

    Today we are sitting around listening to praise music. I need a healing in my body and I know how to get it. I want my healing. I gave Him the cancer and He took it; Now I want to be rid of this pain. Just saying. Because if there is a reason for me to be here and experience this, then I am willing, But I am ready for a break.

    Now, having said that, it is a beautiful day today. Get some friends together and turn the praise music up and let's see if we can generate some heat. Seriously, He dwells in the praises of His people. Praise Him

So much Love He had for Me.
By Ida Helton — Feb 11, 2014 12:27pm

    He loves me. Jesus loves me. He really loves me.

    I have been offline for a few days. Finally decided the only way for the back to heal was to get off my feet, and let God do the work. He is faithful. I can sit up today, which is good. I loaded the dishwasher without major pain. It is working. I just have to give it time.

    Fibromyalgia is my worst enemy and seems to be my partner for life. I have asked God to heal it I have given it to HIM, He is my healer and I praise Him for a job well done. I thank Him because I know I'll be perfect given time.

Much love to all. I love to see you all.

Hallelujah
By Ida Helton — Feb 22, 2014 3:24pm

It's a glorious day. I am sitting in house with doors open, and the dogs and cat are roaming in an out. We are having a quiet day. I met Joe in Irving last night with clean clothes and he turned and left again. We ate at Chubby's in Duncanville, a delicious chicken fried steak dinner.

My carpets are clean, and my kitchen floor is almost to perfection, and my body is screaming out for me to stop. I overdid it by a long shot, now I have to wait for my soreness to go away. But, the carpets are clean. I got a wild hair from somewhere and decided to clean one room. My own shampooer would not work so I had to go rent one, and after paying thirty dollars, I sure wasn't going to take it back to the store without doing my house.

I wore myself out Monday.

The good news here is, I finally (after three years) had enough strength to do some serious cleaning of my own. God has already been so good to me, and my body is recovering, and I am about ready to get going with my life again. God is always good.

Mammogram is NORMAL
By Ida Helton — Mar 18, 2014 12:16pm

I had the yearly mammogram done last month. Now, you may not understand this, but I say and do a lot of things that are contrary to what the enemy says to me. One of the biggest fears for me was that the tumors would still be there. I didn't say it because I don't believe in letting my enemy know where my thoughts go. I speak with my mouth what I want to be true. I proclaim it in Jesus Name, and I bar all interference from Satan.

I am not a name it and claim it person, because I know that sometimes we ask amiss of God's will for us. When we ask amiss, or against His plan for us, He says no. But I personally believe that everything I say with my mouth can come true, therefore I speak no negative. One of the reasons I said I wanted to hear NOTHING NEGATIVE during the battle was because my mind had enough of that all by myself. Bro. Jerry said, "Garbage In, Garbage Out." Absolutely. If I hear negatives they have a chance of coming out my mouth. You can't take that chance when you are fighting for your life.

Now, I did have the thought the mammogram might show a lingering problem. I may always have that thought. But I don't speak it aloud. I hope and trust my friends and family will understand. But then, I dance around the house and praise the Lord loudly when I get the good report. At this time the Mammogram is NORMAL. That's an excellent report.

The Fibromyalgia seems to be responding to rest and sleep, so that, all in all, I am feeling much better today than I was last week.

God has been so good to me. I have a baseball cap in my car. It stays on the dash, so people can see my testimony. GOD HAS BEEN SO GOOD TO ME. And He has.

Thank you all for your prayer and support.

So Blessed.
By Ida Helton — Apr 7, 2014 10:18am

Well, it's Monday, April 7. I am on my way to better health. I have fought a battle that I never dreamed would come. Me. With cancer. Never, in my wildest dreams, did I ever believe it could get me. And yet, here I am. I always thought I had too much faith to let the stuff come near me. That may sound egotistical, but I don't mean it to. I just always thought that my prayers were enough.

Then one day the doctor calls and says, "we need more tests." Suddenly, you are in a vortex, a place where you have never been before. You have to make the choice, quickly, as to whether you have the faith to fight or you lay down and let it run over you.

Next time you see the doctor, "we need to do biopsy." WHAT!!!!! I just got used to this more tests thing, and you want a biopsy. Okay, then, just go ahead. I can handle it. You won't find anything after all. I have prayed all my life for this. This biopsy takes several days for test results, they said. Two days later, all alone and still asleep when the phone rings, "Its Follicular Non-Hodgkin's Lymphoma" And then, because you are talking to a breast cancer specialist, "I don't do Lymphoma, I do breast cancer, we will refer you to oncology."

It's the truth. The doctor said he couldn't answer any questions because he was not an oncologist. Wow, way to leave a girl hanging for a few days. I called Joe. We had already made the decision to face this the same way we handle everything else. PRAYER. It works. I tell him that they are making me an appointment, and he decides to stay home for a week, so he can go with me to Oncologist.

When we first met with Dr. Habte Yimer, he had seen the reports, this was the first sign of anything being in my body, so everyone thought I would be in the early stages. He even told us that it was probably new and was very slow growing, and he would probably watch and wait, to see what would happen. Then he ordered the CT Scan. After talking to him, Joe and I both thought it would be okay if he simply went back to work. He did. We had been in Dr Yimer's office on Wednesday, and he went back to work on Friday morning, leaving me to return to the doctor by myself. When I called him back later, after the consultation, I am told he cried. He didn't let me see that. He called someone else.

STAGE 3. You have Stage 3 Follicular Non-Hodgkin's Lymphoma. There were 4.5 cm tumors in my pelvic area, 3.5 cm tumors in my abdomen, and 1.5 cm tumors all across my chest. I had been sick for a long time. The prognosis was bad. He told me I might only have 3 years to live if they used the chemo they were using at that time, but there is a new one out and if the insurance will approve it, maybe 5 years. The tumors will not go away, they may go into remission, but this cancer is here to stay.

As the doctor was talking, the Holy Spirit came and lifted me up. From the pit of my stomach the Word came out of me. "I sure am glad you didn't write my life story. Jeremiah 29:11 says God knows the plans He has for my life. You can't change or rewrite them. He will work His plan and when it is my time I will go home. He promised me a future." The doctor was rather shocked at my words. But then he said faith was the only thing that would work.

Six months of chemo, two years of maintenance, so many changes in my body. But I never cried. I never let it get to me. I continued to praise God for my healing, and to quote the Word of God over my situation. After three months they did another CT Scan and much to their surprise, the tumors were shrinking. After the six months of chemo they sent me for a PET Scan. The results were amazing. No Cancer, no tumors, nothing in my body would pick up the dye to show them cancer. I am healed.

I still have to do the maintenance every other month. My body is recovering slowly, sometimes too slowly for me, but God is on His Throne, and I am healed by the stripes on Jesus back. I am healed. Totally. I thank God for the work He has done, for what He is doing, and for what will be done.

Recovery and Other Silly Words
By Ida Helton — Apr 19, 2014 9:15pm

It's late on a Saturday night; I have been cancer free for 9 months. I go in every other month and get a treatment of the Rituxan which is supposed to be helping to prevent any return of the cancer. I love the people, I feel so blessed to be at this point of my journey. God has really been there for me and has had His hand on me, and He has brought me through so much in my life. Before I ask, He knows where I am and what it is that I need. He is already there. Already planning, already moving the mountains out of my way, already making the valleys smooth so I can go through without a lot of bumps.

God is God in the mountains, in the valleys, in the good and the bad. He is God. He is always God, and FAITH is Fully And Implicitly Trusting Him.

Family Time for Joe
By Ida Helton — May 4, 2014 3:20pm

I am sitting in a room at the Quality Inn in Greenwood, Indiana. Joe is with his kids and grandkids. I should be with him, but I am in too much pain to make a ride to visit his grandson, Josh, who just got out of the hospital. We came here for his son-in-law's funeral. It was a beautiful celebration of Gary's life and his home going. Not your typical funeral.

I AM A VICTIM OF AMAZING GRACE

We left home at 2:45 in the afternoon, dropped April off with my parents and came on. We stopped for restroom and gasoline. We ate McDonalds in the car on the way. We arrived at the motel at 7:15 am on Saturday morning. After the ride, I am doing good to just walk. I could not get back in the car again today. I told him to go and enjoy his visit. I am beginning to get hungry, so I hope he comes back soon. But if he doesn't, I can always order a pizza or something to eat.

I dread tomorrow because I have to ride back home again in the car. It is very painful and makes me feel so bad. When we get home, I will be back in bed for several days. My body will have to recover again.

God is good to me, and to our family. Joe needed to make peace with this part of his family. I needed to be here for the healing to be complete. We will be a complete family once again. That's what we have prayed for so many years.

I am tired. Will write again later.

I was diagnosed on January 10, 2013, with Follicular Non-Hodgkin's Lymphoma. On the 15th the Oncologist ordered a CT Scan, and then on Fri, the 18th, he told me that it is Stage 3. He ordered a PICC line installed and asked them to start Chemo immediately. I am waiting for insurance approval for that. My story is simple, the doctors didn't write it. God wrote it before I was born. He knows my days, and the hairs on my head. What's a testimony without a test? Just another step on the road to Glory.

Ida Helton
Shared privately - Jan 18, 2013

What a mighty God we serve... Angels bow before Him; Heaven and Earth adore Him. Now, does He want me healed instantly or is there someone watching for my reaction. Here it is. We serve a mighty God and I don't care how He does it or when, so long as He gets the glory. Those who know me know that I cannot do this on my own, but with His help.

I go back to the doctor this afternoon to find out what his final diagnosis is. (Is it fairly new or has it been here for a while) and then he will tell me what treatment plan he has in mind for me. He worked at the Mayo Clinic for 4 years, which really helped me and Awesome Joe to be able to talk to him easier. Thank you, Lord for putting those in my path who will help me and whom I can witness to. I should pray the prayer of Jabez, 'Enlarge my territory, so that I can bless others, and show your Glory all around."

One thing is sure, "He's still in the fire, and He's walking all around, and He'll be there to help you when you call upon His Name. He can still deliver by His Almighty Power. While here below it's good to know He's still in the fire."

Show less
Ida Helton
Jan 21, 2013

Stage 3, Follicular Non-Hodgkin's Lymphoma, Intermediate with tumors up to 4.5 centimeters in my abdomen. PICC line inserted Monday 1/21/13 for Chemo to start (hopefully) tomorrow. Strangest thing, one of the nurses/technicians at the hospital was a spirit filled lady. She prayed with me and was amazed at all that is going on.

These doctors did not write my life story. God wrote it in gold and blood before I was ever born. He has my life planned from the time I am born to the time of death, and He knows exactly how many hairs I have on my head. This didn't just HAPPEN. I have cancer for a reason. If I can change the heart and soul of just one person, then Lord, please use me.

Our God is an Awesome God and I plan to Let Go and Let God.

I AM A VICTIM OF AMAZING GRACE AND…

FAITH IS FULLY AND IMPLICITLY TRUSTING HIM….

www.ingramcontent.com/pod-product-compliance
Ingram Content Group UK Ltd.
Pitfield, Milton Keynes, MK11 3LW, UK
UKHW022214230426
12048UKWH00016BA/836